PREACHING THE
RISEN CHRIST

Hendrickson Preaching Series

PREACHING THE RISEN CHRIST

D. W. CLEVERLEY FORD

HENDRICKSON
PUBLISHERS
PEABODY, MASSACHUSETTS 01961-3473

First published 1988 by Mowbray, a Cassell imprint, London

PREACHING THE RISEN CHRIST

© D. W. Cleverley Ford 1988

Hendrickson Publishers, Inc., Edition 1994

ISBN 1-56563-045-9

Reprinted by arrangement with Mowbray,
an imprint of Cassell plc, London.

Printed in the United States of America

CONTENTS

ACKNOWLEDGEMENTS

May I express my sincere appreciation of the co-operation given me by Miss Barbara Hodge at Canterbury in preparing my manuscript for the publishers, and to the publishers themselves, Messrs A. R. Mowbray & Co. Ltd. of Oxford, for their expertise in production.

Lingfield 1987   D. W. CLEVERLEY FORD

INTRODUCTION

There is an underlying awareness in the community today that we are unlikely to be successful in the art of living together in peace and safety unless we can make the effort to go forward to more Christian standards of private and public conduct than are evident at present. Christian behaviour – and it includes joy as well as self-denial – will not, however, come about in default of Christian faith, and at the heart of Christian faith is the risen Christ. Christianity without Easter is not possible.

We must face the awkward truth, however, that for many Christians, even churchgoers, the resurrection is little more than a problem subject made more so by recent controversy. Of course we enjoy the buoyancy of the Easter hymns, and we fall back on the traditional doctrine when beaten low by bereavement, but the attention we give the resurrection is short-lived. Even Easter sermons quietly cease once the Festival is over, in spite of the fact that every Sunday is supposed to be a weekly reminder of it.

Preaching the Easter gospel is what this book is concerned with. Though alive to the current theological debate it makes no pretence at offering a specific contribution to it. The people in mind are not academics but ordinary worshipping congregations and the preachers who seek to build them up (we trust) in the faith. By and large, congregations have little stomach for theological abstractions, and not much more for history; they are interested in events and they warm to people, but what concerns them most is how to get through the knocking about that life supplies. How can the subject of the risen Christ be opened up for them?

There are preachers, and there are writers, who give the impression that the Easter faith can best be evoked by making the Easter stories conform to a rational, even scientific, interpretation. I doubt it, though I readily recognize that, for some, to be excused from reading those stories as historical narratives but rather as theological interpretations of spiritual reality does allow them to receive the Easter gospel from which they would otherwise feel blocked off.

I do not myself see the Easter stories in the gospels as primarily historical accounts but as testimonies to events which indeed happened, though maybe not exactly as recorded, for there are contradictions in them. What we are provided with are accounts adapted and structured so as to incorporate both testimony to the fact of the resurrection of Jesus and the subsequent experience of the risen Christ. They are artistic representations of events which are only partly explicable. There is mystery here. There is bound to be. We are led up to and beyond the bounds of earthly experience. But if the stories are more like paintings than a record, and accuracy of detail is not the point of the work, complete indifference to accuracy cannot be. A portrait has to be recognizable, but it is more than a photograph, it interprets. In a way it has a message to proclaim. This, as I see the situation, is how the Easter stories in the gospels function, and it is their message, or interpretation of events, which the preacher must relay.

Furthermore, the stories are masterpieces; which being the case, the first necessity is to look carefully at them *as they are.* As with any masterpiece in the Uffizi or National Gallery it is more than likely that details and features will go unobserved unless pointed out by some expert. So the paintings must be displayed and must be commented upon. This is the justification for the resurrection accounts in the gospels being intelligently, and I would say artistically, read in the course of public worship and also *re*-presented in the preaching, lighting up and bringing out the distinctive features. This is where exegesis plays its part and exposition follows, bringing home the message of the narrative as it stands.

This is what I have attempted to do in this book. How far I have succeeded the reader will be able to judge. But I have gone beyond this. I have tried to broaden and deepen the subject because we cannot be content only to light up the Easter stories, nor solely to relate the theme of resurrection to life *after* death. Every one of us has little deaths before then – illness, disappointments, setbacks, even the incidence of retirement – but with the gospel of the risen Christ there can be little resurrections. And Easter has something to say to the community, to the Church, to public morality and to the future. It is to be wondered what part of life and experience it does not touch, so comprehensive is it in its scope.

And what about the preacher? There cannot be preaching without him or her. But is the preacher invariably a visual aid, or an audible aid, to the truth that belief in the risen Christ is life-giving? Even preaching newness of life can be deadly. This is the terror of the pulpit ministry. The preacher may not be, indeed need not be as charismatic as popularly understood, but he must be alive with his message, otherwise stepping down from the pulpit might be the more salutary course of action. To proclaim the risen Christ the preacher must know something of what resurrection is in his/her own experience. This lies beyond the scope of my book but I count it as fundamental.

D. W. C. F.

1. Light out of darkness

1 John 2.8 (RSV) . . . *the darkness is passing away, and the true light already shineth.*

I would like you to see three people in a room together. You will have to use your imagination, but I make no apology. I do not mean wild imagination, I hold no brief for this, but disciplined imagination, imagination which builds reasonably on the information available. If we abjure this, if we stop short with literary criticism only – and do not misunderstand me, I personally owe much to literary criticism of the New Testament – we shall end up with figures like those in Madame Tussaud's in London; wax models with no life in them.

1. Together in the darkness of despair

Three people then, two men and a woman, in a room together. They have no heart left, or scarcely any heart. Yes, they are talking but the conversation is dead. No one expects answers to the questions raised, because during the last twenty-four hours they have lost all hope of answers. Life has sagged down to a heap of inexplicable conundrums. And the fire meant to cheer them has gone out. And the meal on the table is only half eaten; at least, the woman hasn't eaten hers.

I would like you to see the woman first. She is middle-aged, there is grey in her otherwise black hair, and lines on her forehead and at the corners of her mouth, if you look closely. She is a widow and her life, not without its joys, has nevertheless nursed one long puzzle, sometimes painful, and now even the glorious interludes have been drowned in despair. We know nothing of her origin, except that she hailed from the country; but when she was but a girl she knew without a shadow of doubt that God had chosen that through her, indeed through her son, the whole nation would be

1

brought to its proper destiny, and not only they, but all peoples everywhere. Gradually, however, she watched the hopes of the masses of the people, once fired by her son's words and works, fizzle out, not least because he refused to ride on those tempting popular waves. And then jealous men in positions of leadership saw their *status quo* threatened, and so they killed him. What sense could be made now of that initial divine choice of her body to bear this son? Had she been deluded? Was God defeated? But is God God if wicked men can overthrow his purposes? Put yourself in Mary's shoes, for it is of her we speak, Mary the mother of Jesus. But no, you cannot put yourself in Mary's shoes. No one can put himself, or even herself, in Mary's shoes. Hers was a unique calling. Her dejection in that room with those two men was unique. We cannot fathom it. Indeed it is to be wondered if Mary, mother of Jesus, isn't in herself beyond fathoming altogether.

And now I shall have to tell you who were the two men and how all got together in that room. One was John who (it can hardly be doubted) was 'the beloved disciple', so-called; and the other was Peter, Simon Peter, also an apostle. The place was John's house in Jerusalem and the time was Easter Eve. We have precise information how Mary and John were there. Before his end came on the cross, Jesus had commended these two to each other. 'Behold thy mother', he said to John, 'and from that hour the disciple took her to his own home' (John 19.27). If we use our imagination, for which I have asked, we can see the young man's arm through Mary's as they trudge their own *via dolorosa* back from the crucifixion site into the city to his house which was cold and hollow, as the whole heaven and earth felt to them as they opened the door.

But John did not stay. Poor Mary! He returned to the crucifixion to witness the closing scene which Mary was spared. He heard the final words. He saw the final breath. His attention, however, was captured by a man in the watching crowd. No, I cannot prove it, but this is how it seems to me. His face was working. His eyes were pools of dark misery. Remorse was devouring him. He would go mad if someone did not rescue him. Perhaps his mind was on the nearby potter's field with its empty clay pits where Judas had already ended his life. This was Simon Peter. And so John slipped his arm through Peter's, as he had through Mary's, and took him home, weeping all the way. That is how all three came to be together. And that is how Peter and John were able to run together to the tomb of Jesus early in the morning.

2. Where love avails

What I have been describing is the prelude to Easter. It is a dark prelude couched in despair. But light broke in. It broke in gradually, even in an unexpected fashion. It was already breaking in with a little group of women already stealing along the darkened streets. They were on their way to perform properly what the men who buried Jesus did fumblingly – to anoint the beloved body with costly perfumes and more costly tears. They were not impelled by any form of intellectual or theological inquiry. This is not how the light of Easter most commonly breaks in. They were acting, in their own way, out of love, but they did not lose their reward. The first appearance of the risen Christ was to one of these women, Mary Magdalene.

We shall be wise to pause here and reflect. Women can teach us about the deep areas of life as no man can teach us. They can do for us what no male can do. When we are growing children it is women who have the care of us. When we are ill it is women who nurse us. Forgive me if at this point I draw on my experience scarcely more than twelve months past. It took place on the third or fourth night, I cannot recall which, after a major surgical operation. I lay on my hospital bed, an agonized heap of scorching pain, struggling unsuccessfully not to cry like a child, my resistance gone. I felt ashamed. Then, unexpectedly, I was aware of a face looking down on me, a kindly woman's face. I read the name on her nurse's uniform, but it meant nothing except that she was married. Without a word she took me, somehow, in her arms, my head on her bosom, rocking me and soothing me as if I were her little boy, until, I suppose, the pain-killing injection began to do its work. Then tenderly she laid me back on the bed and departed. About two weeks later I saw her again. I suppose it was her turn of duty. I thanked her for what she had done for me, and apologized for not putting up 'a better show'. All she did was to smile sweetly and walk away. I never saw her again, but several times I have said to myself, 'Thank God for women'. No man, no male nurse, however competent, could have done what she did for me that night. I shall not forget.

Women can teach us that love opens doors no intellectual expertise can open. Mary Magdalene encountered the risen Christ before anyone else, not because she was more intelligent and had more theological equipment to boast than anyone else but *because she loved*. Let no one reckon because he/she is no scholar and remains unmoved by academic study of the New Testament that the risen Christ is not for them. The intellectual debate about the resurrection of Jesus will go on till the end of time, and few will be the better for it. Meanwhile, the risen Christ will make himself known to those who love the little or much they see of him in the gospels, the Christian fellowship and the Christlikeness of some ordinary men and women they know. It is a lesson to be treasured from the action of the women on Easter Sunday morning which gives encouragement to us all.

3. *Where reason avails and does not avail*

We must also see, however, that reason has its place in Christian discipleship. Come back to that room where the three are mourning, two men and a woman. The time is early on Easter Sunday morning. Perhaps they are scarcely awake. More likely, they have never slept. Suddenly a hammering on the door, an insistent hammering. It is Mary Magdalene breathless. She has run from the garden tomb to the city with the frightening news that the sepulchre is empty, the precious body has been removed. So Peter and John are brought to their feet and they too run. They cannot reach the grave soon enough.

And now we turn to the fourth gospel itself, to chapter 20, and read how John arrived first and did not enter, but Peter had no hesitation and he went straight in. Observe now the difference between these two men. Both saw the same strange sight, the tomb empty and the grave clothes undisturbed. Clearly no thieves had been at work. Only John, however, read a meaning in what he saw. Only for him did the sight set a light to a conviction dormant in him since Galilean days that Jesus was no ordinary man but Son of God, who of course was life itself and could not be defeated by a human death. And when these two went home, as we are told they did, John was in heaven but Peter was in hell, no matter what John reasoned. Peter was no thinker, he was all heart, or nearly all heart and very little head; reason played but the smallest part in his devotion. This was his disadvantage. It is always a disadvantage if we cannot, or will not, give our minds to what we believe. But this has to be said loud and clear. Had Peter all the brains of the most erudite Rabbi in Jerusalem it would have helped but little in his condition then. His trouble was not intellectual. What drove him down to hell was the thought that Christ might be risen for John, but he would never be risen for him, for had he not cut him when the pace grew hot in the high priest's palace and Jesus stood on trial? Was he not an outcast for ever? How could he return to the house to be with Mary the Mother of Jesus, and John, the beloved disciple? How could he settle anywhere? How could he do anything but hide in misery till death gave him a merciful release? But he did not have to hide. No one has to hide from the risen Christ, whatever his sins, if he is truly sorry. Peter, to his utter astonishment, found this out, and he could never get over the wonder of it. The risen Christ appeared to him all on his own with forgiveness and restoration. It was life to a dying man. Where it happened no one knows but this is the fact to grasp with both our hands; this appearance to this unworthy ordinary man became *the great event* of the apostolic preaching of the risen Christ. See it set out in St Paul's first letter to the Corinthians, chapter 15. It connects the risen Christ with forgiveness. This is the good news, this is the gospel, and it is music to our ears; or, as the Authorized Version words, the text with which we began, 'the darkness is past, and the true light now shineth'.

2. A Bereavement Transformed

John 20.17 (NEB) *Jesus said, 'Do not cling to me, for I have not yet ascended to the Father. But go to my brethren, and tell them that I am now ascending to my Father and your Father, my God and your God.'*

A little while ago I was brought into contact with a woman recently bereaved of her husband. People were kind to her; they wrote letters of sympathy; they invited her out to meals to help combat her inevitable loneliness; and her sons, though living at a distance, were assiduous in telephoning her from time to time. She put up a brave show and, (as we say), managed 'to get along'. But I recall a thought I had vividly at the time; suppose, just suppose, her late husband suddenly appeared in the doorway! She would be swept off her feet. She would cling to him in her arms unable to let him go.

1. *What Mary lost*

Something similar happened to Mary Magdalene on Easter morning. No, of course she had not lost a husband, but it is possible for a man to be all the world to a woman although she is not married to him, nor does any thought of such a relationship even enter the picture. But Mary Magdalene was a woman, and therefore love was part of her being. I have sometimes wondered if she was by temperament akin to the type Jane Austen represented in her novel *Sense and Sensibility* in the person of Marianne – romantic, precipitate, intense, a women by no means devoid of reasoning powers but powerfully impelled by passion. And Mary Magdalene possessed good grounds for being drawn to the man Jesus of Nazareth. Had he not lifted her up from a life of shame, implanting within her the conviction of her own worth before God and therefore before other people, and given her a joy in her heart she had never known before?

7

But now she had lost him. Worse still she had actually watched him being killed, slowly, cruelly and before the gloating eyes of a callous crowd. And when they took his body down from the cross she noted the place where they laid it. Are you surprised that within twenty-four hours she was visiting the site, gazing, you may guess, through her fast-flowing tears at the forbidding stone which stopped all entry to the sepulchre? Are you surprised that the Sabbath, now being technically ended, she was at the shops seeking precious spices to anoint the sacred body? And are you surprised that next morning, Easter morning, before the sun was up (according to the fourth gospel) she was already making for the garden tomb beyond the city wall, anxious to perform all that was left for her feminine hands to perform, now that he was dead?

There was, however, nothing she could do. No corpse was there. The tomb was empty – so the records say. Aghast, she ran back into the city. Women, especially Eastern women, do not run, except under compulsion, and only then if they are young. Mary Magdalene, we are specifically told, ran to break her anguished report to the disciples, 'They have taken away the Lord out of his tomb and we do not know where they have laid him'. Mourning and crying though they were (see Mark 16.10) Peter and John of their number set off to see for themselves, also at a run. They did see, and, in their haste to break the news, made for the city, giving no thought to Mary back again at the sepulchre, the tears streaming down her face. Four times over, the Johannine account mentions those tears.

And then it happened. A man was standing close behind her. 'Mary!' he said. She could not believe her ears. No one spoke her name as he spoke it. It was Jesus, the man she'd lost, lost she thought for ever. Are you surprised that she moved to throw her arms around him? What woman in like circumstances would do otherwise?

This is amazing! A woman's name, tenderly spoken, is actually the first recorded word of the risen Christ! Can you believe it? I recommend that you do believe it for there is strong consolation here. Then, gently no doubt, but firmly, he headed her off. '*Noli tangere*', 'Do not touch me'. Jesus had not come back through the door of Mary's life to resume the old relationship of human fellowship. Mary had lost him at that level of association. Death blocks it off. Whatever hopes we may hold, and rightly hold, of resurrection, the hurt of bereavement is not abolished. The Easter gospel does not at once dry up those tears. It cannot.

We must not be taken aback therefore that the first recorded utterance of the risen Christ over and above Mary's name was a prohibition: 'Do not cling to me'. Mary must know, and we must learn, that Easter offers no mere replay of our earthly mode of existence but life of another order, not only more glorious, but without tears, without partings and without pain. We may be sure Mary Magdalene found this hard to appreciate as do we all at times. But we must lay hold of this hope. Easter does not cancel out bereavement but it does transform it. We lose through the incidence of death as Mary lost, but what she and we gain is, and will be, infinitely greater.

2. What we gain

And now listen to the probition again; 'Do not cling to me'. We are not to cling to the earthly man of Nazareth as if such clinging constituted the core of Christianity: it does not – which does not mean that the story of Jesus can be discounted. There never has been, there never will be, anything like it. Without it we have no foundation for the Christian gospel. Christianity is a historical religion, that is to say, it is grounded in history, grounded in events which took place, and Jesus of Nazareth at the centre of them. But Christianity in essence is more than admiration of a superb teacher, a compassionate healer, an obedient servant to the will of God, even a man to be dearly loved; though he was all of these and more. Such is an extremely limited view of Christ. It puts him into the category of Plato, Alexander the Great, Charlemagne and Napoleon, men utterly diverse but, at one in this, that they altered the course of history. And so did Jesus.

We must not cling to his influence on history as if this were all, however. The historical life of Jesus was preparatory to a wider ministry by far, indeed, to an unlimited ministry. At his resurrection his restriction by space and time to Galilee and Judaea was done away. Henceforth he was available to men and women far beyond the confines of touch and sight. So now his is a universal spiritual presence, no less real, no less close, no less concerned for everything about us, and on Easter morning he appeared to Mary Magdalene to assure her of precisely these things. She must not cling to the past, she must move on to the more glorious present and future. Herein is to be found the core of Christianity; *communion with the spiritual presence of Christ*, as available in AD 1989 as in AD 29. The stage of adoring love such as Mary's, bitter in bereavement, is basically transformed: Christ is now one to whom we pray. Herein lies the difference.

3. What we must all give

And now the text once more: Jesus said 'Do not cling to me . . . go to my brothers'. Do not these last four words cause us to catch our breath? 'Go to my brothers.' Here is the risen Christ, here is the Christ shortly to ascend to the Father to be seated in glory – symbolic words, to be sure, but what other words are available for so utterly unique an occasion? Yet here he is associating himself still with eleven very ordinary men, the leader of whom was a fisherman! He acknowledges them as 'brothers', brothers of Christ!

So the risen Christ does not forget us, indeed he is risen and will ascend to glory *for us*. 'In my Father's house are many mansions . . . I go to prepare a place for you.' Isn't this, according to St John, what he said the night before his crucifixion? Christ owns us. This is the staggering thought. He owns us even before we own him. Thus the invitation of the

Easter gospel is to accept that divine ownership. We are the brethren, we are the brothers and sisters of Christ if we will accept ownership of us as such. Can we believe it?

Here is a gospel to proclaim, and Mary must set about it at once; 'Go to my brothers and tell them'. Privilege carries with it responsibility. And the last we see of Mary is of this young woman running (I cannot believe she sauntered) back to the disciples, her eyes shining bright, 'I have seen the Lord'. Did they believe her? Would you have believed her? Do we believe her now? This is still the sharp Easter question. On our answer depends whether or not what we have is the real Christian faith.

3. To Heal the Broken-hearted

Luke 24.34 (NEB) *It is true: the Lord has risen; he has
appeared to Simon.*

You must speak this verse out loud. You can't just read it. But
you can't speak it out loud properly unless your heart beats as a
Christian; though you might just do so if you are a born actor,
then you might get the accent right and put some excitement
into it; for make no mistake, excitement there still is, hanging
all about it, deriving from that evening behind closed doors
when it was first uttered. It was a corporate utterance, a
spontaneous corporate utterance. That is to say, ten men
voiced it together, or almost together. I guess they were
jumping up and down, their eyes bright with amazement and
bewilderment. When Cleopas and his companion burst into
the room, buoyant if battered from all they had gone through
on the journey to Emmaus and back, the ten men they greeted
countered their excitement with their own mounting enthusi-
asm, 'It is true, the Lord has risen!' But that was not all. 'He
has appeared to Simon.' To *Simon*! Can you believe it? The
Lord has appeared to the man who, under pressure, disowned
him! At which moment, you can be sure, all eyes swivelled to
Simon.

There are some sermons I tremble to preach but not this
one. No, I am not going to dramatize myself like some of those
'born again' Christians who in their 'testimonies' pile on
the luridness of their pre-conversion past, supplying a stun-
ning story. I have nothing lurid to disclose, nor for that matter
to hide. But at the back of me, I regret to say, there lies a great
deal of sheer ordinariness, moments of doubt about the whole
Christian 'thing', occasions when I could have behaved better
than I did, resentments and moroseness which were quite
unjustified. These are denials of the Christ I profess to preach.
But, you see, the risen Lord appeared to Simon who avowed in
the courtroom when his Master was on trial for his life, 'I do
not know the man'. Shame on you Simon! But if Simon could

12

be forgiven, if Simon was not dropped, if Simon was the first to whom the risen Christ appeared on that first Easter Day, need I be dropped? Need you be dropped? Need that scoundrel round the corner, if he is truly sorry and repents, be dropped? I tell you, I, with all my unworthiness, do not tremble to preach this sermon. I want to shout it from the house tops. 'It is true: the Lord has risen; he has appeared to *Simon*.'

1. Peter the intimate

Let me tell you about Simon Peter. He had been a fisherman, earning his living as a fisherman, but Jesus of Nazareth called him away from it. So he became one of the twelve disciples; which did not mean simply that he formed part of Jesus' *entourage*, but that he was a companion of Jesus, even an intimate, sharing his thoughts, his concerns, even his temptations (see Luke 22.28). We've got it all wrong if we think of Jesus as existing in Galilee and Judaea in magisterial isolation. Jesus was a man, a real human being, and human beings must have human fellowship to be human and remain human. Is it surprising then that we read in Mark 3.14 that Jesus called his disciples not only that he might send them out to preach but simply that they might *be with him*? And suppose Papias' written statement in the early part of the second century AD has truth in it that St Mark's Gospel was based on the reminiscences of Simon Peter, who would know of this intimacy with Jesus more than he? So I stress this point, Simon Peter was very close to Jesus and Jesus was very close to Simon Peter.

2. Peter the failure

But Simon let Jesus down. He let him down on what we call Maundy Thursday evening. Jesus was in the High Priest's palace on trial for his life and Peter could not endure to think of him there alone. So, with his fellow-disciple John, he dared to infiltrate into this hotbed of hostility. Let us be fair to Peter. He was not lacking in courage and what flamed it was his devotion. Devotion can do this. Think what women have braved in defence of their loved ones! But Peter's courage snapped, humiliatingly it snapped with the accusation of a woman, a serving maid, looking into his face: 'You were there too,' she said 'with this man from Nazareth, this Jesus.' Peter feigned ignorance of what she was talking about and said so, but so alerted was he to danger he removed to the porch. The girl watched him out there and remarked to the bystanders 'He is one of them'. Again Peter denied it. Not long afterwards he was confronted again, this time by the bystanders; 'Surely you are one of them. You must be; you are a Galilean.' Poor Peter. It was too much. His courage collapsed in a heap. Cursing and with an oath he blurted out 'I do not know this man you speak of'. Now was the time to cut and run. Peter did cut and run, but not before he heard a distant cock crow, lacerating his soul with the memory of Jesus' prophesy to him not half a dozen hours since, 'Before the cock crows twice you will deny me thrice'. Peter ran, the tears streaming down his tough, weather-beaten face; ran, you may be sure, into hiding, his heart broken. He had made a mess of his discipleship. What future for him now? His Master would drop him.

And now my text from Luke 24.34: 'It is true: the Lord has risen; he has appeared to *Simon*'. You see now why I do not tremble to preach this particular sermon. It gives me a chance. It gives you a chance. It gives every sinner a chance. There is no wrong that we can do, have done, or will do that can, if we repent of it and possibly even suffer cruelly for it, forever shut us out from the Lord's presence, even from his service. The Lord appeared to Simon after his resurrection. He did not drop him. He had him back.

My mind goes away to a particular situation many years ago. I had a friend whom we nicknamed Ginger, a sturdily built young man who was a Bachelor of Science when I met him and a good hockey player. He got ordained, but not long after made a mess of his ministry. No, not on account of some lurid transgression; he did not run off with his vicar's wife or anything of that kind. What happened was that when he started to preach to others his own unworthiness overcame him. Perhaps his thoughts were not always clean (but whose are?); I do not know. But whatever his trouble was he lost his grip: his marriage suffered and he sailed away alone to South America where he wasn't known, hoping to start afresh. But of course his plan failed. You can't sail away from your soul, to South America or anywhere else. You have to listen to the gospel, and perhaps to its embodiment in my text 'It is true: the Lord has risen; he has appeared to Simon'. Yes, to Simon! If only Ginger could have let this gospel save him. If only someone could have presented it!

3. Peter the restored

And now we turn our attention to Easter Sunday morning, just after daybreak. There was no hope anywhere among the disciples and followers of Jesus. They'd seen the man they thought might be the Messiah crucified. Would they ever erase the ghastly scene from their minds? And now his grave stood in a garden outside Jerusalem's city wall as a monument to a disastrous failure. The disciples lay low. Who wouldn't lie low? But one woman, with one or two others, crept out; not to see, but to anoint the beloved body with funeral ointments. Horror hit them however. No corpse was there. But they were soon hurrying back to the city with a story of resurrection spoken to them by an angel. Breathlessly they told it to Peter and John (for they knew where they were hiding). Did the men believe the women? Put yourself in their shoes: put yourself in Simon Peter's shoes. Would you believe their story? All the same Peter hurried with John to the burial place. Perhaps he reckoned the sight of it might soothe his sorely scarred soul. Perhaps he thought that, with his mind tugged this way and that with shame and perplexity, to be up and doing was preferable to sitting still, brooding. Who is there who does not know the feeling? When he reached the tomb however, and looking in saw the linen clothes lying there but no body, what he saw did not speak to him of resurrection. He was too broken, too numb in mind to see anything more than further evidence of failure. Even the body was gone. Simon Peter simply went back to his hiding place to brood.

And then it happened. Where it happened we do not know, neither have we access to any details of what took place. All we know is that the risen Christ appeared to Simon, all by himself. But the event was so important the record of its having taken place became part of the basic Christian proclamation. When in his letter to the Corinthians (1 Cor. 15.3-7) St Paul listed the facts that were imparted to him within less than half a dozen years after the crucifixion and resurrection of Jesus, prominent among them was the appearance to Simon Peter. The women's story was not mentioned. What Cleopas and his companion experienced on the road to Emmaus was not mentioned, nor the miraculous draft of fishes on the Galilean lake after the resurrection. It was not that these events had not taken place, but they did not compare in importance with the fact that after the resurrection Christ first appeared to Simon Peter, who was the leading apostle but who had let him down. The gospel, the good news for sinners is explicit there as nowhere else. The risen Christ's first work is to restore the broken-hearted.

4. A story

I do not know that there is anything I can add to this, so let me end with a story. It is about Alfred Dreyfus, a Frenchman of Jewish descent born in Mulhouse in 1859. He came to hold a post of some importance in the War Ministry; and there never was a more hardworking, diligent and devoted servant of France than he. Not infrequently he worked long into the night at his office desk to have documents ready for the next day where others took days, if not weeks, to prepare the material. Jealousy crept in however, coupled with anti-semitism – never far below the surface in France. Dreyfus found himself charged with betraying military secrets to Germany. Court-martialled and pronounced guilty he was banished to Devil's Island: this was in 1894. What degrada-tion, privation and misery he suffered in that hideous place was brought home to the British public a few years ago in a moving film. We saw this sensitive man formally stripped of his medals on a military parade ground; and we saw his devastated wife worn with pretending to their children that daddy had been sent on special war work overseas. But the truth got out, and that great French writer, Emile Zola, would not let it be hidden: it was Major Esterhazy who had betrayed military secrets to Germany, not Dreyfus. So a retrial was held in 1899 at which Dreyfus was pronounced guilty with extenuating circumstances and received a pardon. But this wasn't good enough. For seven long years his champions fought for his innocence till a Court of Appeal in 1906 pronounced him free of all guilt; and at a public ceremony his medals were pinned on him again. He had been broken but he was restored. It was right, a thousand times right. Dreyfus had done nothing wrong. But what shall we say of Simon Peter? That he was innocent? He knew he wasn't. When it came to the crunch he denied his Master, he disowned the eternal Son of God with curses and oaths in a public place. But that same Son of God, risen and glorified, restored him to his place and ministry because he genuinely repented. That is the Christian gospel. It really is. 'It is true: the Lord has risen; he has appeared to *Simon.*'

4. The Sight was the Message

John 20.20 *Then were the disciples glad when they saw the Lord.*

There is no verse in the Bible more lame than this; perhaps 'inept' would be more appropriate. 'Then were the disciples glad when they saw the Lord.' As lame and inept might it be said of those women lining the docks at Southampton at the conclusion of the Falklands War, straining their eyes to catch the first glimpse of the returning troop ships entering the harbour, each woman agog to see if this man, that man, up there on the deck, the rigging or the gun turrets really was her man – could you possibly merely say, 'they were pleased to see their husbands?' Or someone like Madam Sakharov, if not Madam Sakharov herself, actually seeing her husband come back from the living hell of a Soviet labour camp, 'She was glad to greet him once again'? These expressions won't do! Those disciples were mad with excitement when they saw the Lord in the room where they were hiding behind bolted doors. They were jumping up and down. They were, I shouldn't wonder, rolling on the floor in uncontrollable exhilaration. There are circumstances in which men do just that. You don't believe me? Well, read what happened when news began to filter through to the prisoner-of-war camps in Germany during the last war that the second front had been started! So in that room on the first Easter Day where the disciples had imprisoned themselves; you can be sure tears of joy were coursing down their cheeks when 'they saw the Lord'. Curious, I know, how we cry when we are overjoyed, but we do. I guess all those disciples were 'weeping buckets' (as we say) when 'they saw the Lord'.

1. Jesus the extraordinary man

First let me say this. You and I will never understand the Christian religion unless we get within our sights the adoration

18

in which the first disciples of Jesus held him. I know, as you know, that marvellous refrain in Handel's *Messiah*, and the equally marvellous contralto solo which carries it – 'a man of sorrows and acquainted with grief'. I confess I never hear it without having to check hard on my emotions. But do you think for one moment that that phrase, however apt as a description of Jesus on the cross, could be written across the whole life of Jesus of Nazareth as people knew him? Do you imagine that twelve men, all of them young, all of them energetic, all of them eager for life, would follow a man of sorrows up hill and down dale, as they did, sharing their meals, roughing it with him on their journeys, witnessing the open-mouthed astonishment with which the crowds hung upon his words and gasped at his works of healing, if that is all he was?

No, Jesus was an extraordinary man; so strong physically, so quick, so intelligent, so unbelievably unflappable, and excellent company. Given equality of circumstances, there wasn't a man in Galilee or Judaea who could stand by him in comparison; not Caiaphas, not Pilate, not Herod Antipas, nor in the Roman Empire itself. Why do you think the authorities of his day were 'hell bent' (as we say) on getting rid of him? Because he was a rival! Sometimes I think we read these stories in the gospels as if the figures in them were made of cardboard. But they were alive, as you and I are alive, perhaps more so. All of which means that the disciples adored this extraordinary man Jesus whom they called 'Master'. Unless we see this we shall never even sense the blinding misery of these men when they saw *this Jesus* crucified outside Jerusalem's walls where the dung hills were, killed by men who were unfit even to untie the laces of his sandals.

But then, when all was over; or in their reckoning all was over, they 'saw the Lord' standing in their midst. Can you believe it? Does anyone believe it? Did the disciples believe it? They had to believe it. So this is the fact which comes out of it all – the Christian religion has its roots in spontaneous adoration of the man Jesus of Nazareth. No one is able to be a

Christian without being stirred by him. Jesus is striking. I doubt if we can understand the vitality of our Christian origins unless we grasp something of how extraordinary the man Jesus of Nazareth was, and living in our world.

2. Jesus the risen and marred Christ

Come back to the text, 'Then were the disciples glad when they saw the Lord'. Notice these last four words, 'they saw the Lord'. What they *saw* was more significant than what they heard: the message lay in what the Lord looked like. It had been so in Galilee and Judaea; his appearance reinforced his words. What was it then that they saw in the locked room on Easter Day? The risen Christ, yes. But there was no fanfare of trumpets, no sceptre in his hand, no escorting legions of angels, not even one angel, and no halo around his head.

When we church people make our way through what we call the Christian year, almost unconsciously we sit back when Lent is over and Good Friday is past and Easter has been triumphantly observed. Christ has left all that tension, strife and pain of our world behind, and is entered into his glory, so different from all that has gone before. But has he? Has he left all the joy and sorrow, all the pleasure and pain – or to employ a comprehensive word, has he abandoned for ever all *the humanity* of this earthly life? But nothing about his appearance, risen Christ though he was and entered into his glory, nothing proclaimed that message. The disciples saw the Jesus they knew before them, only he was risen from the grave. And then, driving home the message into their hearts and minds for ever, they observed the wound marks on his body; they could scarcely take their eyes off them. What they saw was a *marred* risen Christ.

What does this mean? That Jesus rose with identification marks upon him? Yes, the crucifixion wounds were that for one apostle, Thomas. They rubbed out his doubts concerning the identity of the figure before him, making him cry out 'My

Lord and my God'. But the wound marks were more than identification labels for doubters. They tell us, as no words could tell us more plainly, that the sufferings of this world, the cries of the distressed since the world began and until it ends, are echoed always in the very heart of God in heaven itself. God suffers because we suffer. He is a compassionate God, he suffers *with* (this is what the word means). So the cross of Christ is not only an event in history, it is a proclamation of what God is like for all eternity. When the disciples saw the crucifixion marks on the *risen* Christ (please note *risen* Christ), they had before them the wherewithal to come to this astonishing truth about God.

Yes, I know this is hard to believe. A few days ago three men escaped unhurt from a burning house; they believed it to be God's deliverance. But then six million Jews perished in the holocaust, some of them children tossed into the incinerators without first being gassed. Oh God, why? Such faith as we have can never be anything else but a struggle in the face of the age-long miseries of so much of the human race. Yet if we have no sight of the *marred* risen Christ we have no light at all for the dark places of our earthly pilgrimage.

There are those who seem to reckon that a sight of Jesus as the man of Galilee is sufficient guide for the life we have to live. I am the last person to minimize attention to this extraordinary figure; nevertheless, unless we also see him risen our encounter with him could lead to despair, for without the resurrection what can our deduction be but that the good life, even the very best, runs down in the end to nothing but defeat by death? Perhaps this is why St Paul wrote in that famous fifteenth chapter of I Corinthians on the resurrection, 'If in this life only we have hoped in Christ we are of all men most pitiable', which is to say 'If we have hoped in Christ in his earthly life only as the man of Nazareth, and not also in his resurrected life, we are of all men most pitiable'. (The Greek could be read this way.) No one knew this better than the disciples in the bolted room on the evening of Easter Day, which is why, when they saw the Lord *risen*, they were glad;

only I believe they jumped up and down with uncontrollable joy.

3. Telling simplicity

What the disciples saw was more telling than what Jesus said. This is the point I have been making. Isn't it true that the television is more influential for most people than is sound radio? People remember what they see. So after his resurrection we do not read in the gospels of sermons Jesus preached, only of appearances he made. He was determined that the image of his risen-ness should be firmly fixed in their minds.

Nevertheless Jesus did speak when he appeared in that barred and bolted room, but it was so simple, so ordinary, the disciples must have questioned their hearing. He said 'Good evening' – at least words of greeting just as commonplace – *Shalom* – 'Peace be with you'. It was what everybody said to anybody in the street, and still do in Jerusalem. '*Shalom*, peace be with you.' Actually, he said it twice. There was no mistaking the words. It must have made the disciples feel like old times again. Nothing grand, nothing lordly, but everything simple and ordinary at their level; and for that reason not less memorable but more so.

Some fifteen years ago a simple and very ordinary act made such an impression on me I have never forgotten it. I was in hospital in the casualty ward. Into the bed opposite mine was brought a boy aged about twelve requiring a sudden appendix operation. After his parents left him he was scared. I heard him crying into his pillow. I slipped out of bed and went and sat by him. I talked. I got the boy to talk. Never was my meagre repertoire of conversation about bicycles, football, aeroplanes and railway engines so exhausted. But it worked. When his minuscule supper arrived he ate it and fell asleep. Next morning they operated. He quickly recovered, and his parents after a few days called to fetch him home. At the door of the ward the boy hesitated, looked across to my bed, fumbled in his pocket and came and gave me a sweet. That was fifteen years ago. I have not forgotten. It shows how memorable a simple act can be.

Come back with me to the room where on the evening of Easter Day the disciples of Jesus were locked 'for fear of the Jews', as St John says, but where the risen Christ suddenly appeared and as suddenly vanished. I fancy I can hear those men whispering 'Did you hear what he said?' He simply said 'Good evening', and he simply looked as in the old days. Did I say 'simply'? – but it is the simple and the little things we remember. They are sometimes the bearer of huge lessons. They were that evening in the room where 'the disciples were glad when they saw the Lord'.

5.   I Can't Take It

John 20.25 (RSV) *So the other disciples told him, 'We have seen the Lord.' But he said to them, 'Unless I see in his hands, the print of the nails, and place my finger in the mark of the nails, and place my hand in his side, I will not believe.'*

Today I propose telling a story. It is not my story but St John's story – there were many other stories he might have told about the resurrection of Jesus and how his disciples reacted to it but he decided to select this one about Thomas, doubting Thomas as he is so often called, because it was a story in which his hearers might recognize themselves; that certainly is why I propose retelling it now.

1. *A melancholy type*

Thomas was not one of those happy-go-lucky men, always talking, always joking, ready to tell a funny tale at the drop of a hat, excellent company in the bar, not shy to slap anyone on the shoulder and generous with everybody's foibles because generous with his own; the type whom no one takes too seriously but who helps to make the party go. Poor Thomas, he couldn't cope with that sort, he would have to sit in a corner and say nothing.

Truth to tell, Thomas was a melancholy man. His genes made him a melancholy man, and to that extent he could not help his melancholy, but I guess there were circumstances as well. Life had not worked out well for Thomas. Not that he hadn't tried. God knows he had tried hard enough, but nothing seemed to work out for him. His counterpart in today's world would be the honest and capable worker who gets made redundant, whose house develops dry rot and whose friends to whom he has given his heart let him down. Thomas is the kind of man who always fears the worst, and to whom the worst always seems to happen, possibly because he fears it. 'Poor old Thomas', we say, 'a gloomy fellow, never sees the

24

bright side, some days he'd turn the milk sour by merely looking at it.'

Be careful, however, how you write him off. Thomas may be melancholy but he has depth, that is partly why he is as he is. Thomas is a man with ideals and it hurts him to observe how ill they fit with our sordid, grumbling world. Thomas is a man sensitive to beauty and responsive to love. Get close to him and he will stick closer than a brother. Above all else he longs to believe and trust and hope, and wishes he could, but he can't always; hence his wry jokes when he troubles to utter them. You must read between the lines of this man's apparent cynicism. It exists because he has been hurt in his passage through life. His doubts are the index of his sensitivity. Thomas is a man not to hate, but to love; not to push out, but to pull in, and, if you do he will stay by your side till his dying day.

Not long ago I came across these lines of that sad little lady Christina Georgina Rossetti, 1830–1894; and when I thought about them I wondered if she were not the counterpart of Thomas: could he have written them or something like them?

> When I am dead, my dearest,
> Sing no sad songs for me;
> Plant thou no roses at my head,
> Nor shady cypress tree:
> Be the green grass above me
> With showers and dewdrops wet;
> And if thou wilt, remember,
> And if thou wilt forget.
>
> I shall not see the shadows,
> I shall not feel the rain;
> I shall not hear the nightingale
> Sing on, as if in pain;
> And dreaming through the twilight
> That doth not rise nor set,
> Haply I may remember,
> And haply may forget.

I think Rossetti's song was a song Thomas might have sung as I shall now show you from the New Testament.

2. *Three disclosures of Thomas*

(a) Thomas the melancholy man was chosen to be an apostle. That in itself is worth noting. His name is bracketed with Matthew in the gospel of St Matthew, and one wonders how on earth these two rubbed along together (if they ever did), supposing that Matthew is identical with Levi the tax-gatherer who, to be a tax-gatherer must have been pretty slick. But we never hear of Thomas till almost the close of the Lord's ministry. Judging by the records he never said anything significant till then. And how melancholy when he did utter, oh, so melancholy. His fellow disciples had been attempting to turn Jesus back from journeying to Jerusalem because they knew the hostility of that place towards him, 'Rabbi, the Jews were but now seeking to stone you, and are you going there again?' And how did Thomas respond? How would you expect? He resigned himself to the worst. 'Let us also go that we may die with him.' Melancholy perhaps, or 'Dismal Jimmy', however you describe his type, but we must not overlook his intense devotion. Thomas would rather be dead than go on living without his Master. And you can be sure that love of his was all mixed up with puzzled bewilderment at the strangeness of this extraordinary man from Nazareth whom he had agreed to follow.

(b) And so we come to the second recorded utterance of Thomas in the gospel of St John. In the Upper Room, the night before his death, Jesus had been saying those words which have sustained the hearts and minds of millions down the ages, 'Let not your hearts be troubled; believe in God, believe also in me. In my Father's house are many rooms; if it were not so would I have told you that I go to prepare a place for you? And when I go and prepare a place for you, I will come again and will take you to myself that where I am you may be also. And you know the way where I am going.' But Thomas' heart definitely *was* troubled. He couldn't make sense of what Jesus was saying. It did not seem logical. If we are not informed clearly of the destination how can we possibly know the way to it? He said so in no uncertain terms: 'Lord, we do not know where you are going, how can we know the way?'

(c) And now the third event in the story of Thomas as the New Testament unveils it. The time is only some days after the resurrection of Jesus. Thomas is protesting almost brutally against the joyful testimony of his fellow disciples that they had seen the Lord; 'Unless I see in his hands the print of the nails, and place my finger in the mark of the nails, and place my hand in his side, I will not believe'. So what Thomas was demanding as a prelude to faith was visible and tangible proof of the resurrection. I called it an almost brutal protest because it was made to men who were overjoyed with what they had experienced, and to have cold water poured then is harsh. But then life had been harsh with Thomas. So many hopes had been dashed, so many loves trampled on, so many apparent opportunities had turned out to be dead ends, that he couldn't take any more, wouldn't risk any more. Hence his stubborn refusal to join in with the disciples' joy, 'Unless I see . . . I will not believe.'

3. The climax of faith

But see why Thomas missed the thrilling experience of the risen Christ standing in their midst which the other disciples had enjoyed. It was because he had absented himself from their company. This is one of the troubles of the melancholy types. They will go off on their own and so miss what can only come to people assembled together. Those who count church-going unimportant please note. It is in the believing community assembled for worship that faith is likely to be evoked. Something happens there which has little to do with logic and argument. We can't make it happen and we can't guarantee it will happen, but the possibility is always there. This is what Thomas missed.

But see how the other disciples talked Thomas round. They must have had their work cut out, but there he was with them at their next assembly behind closed doors. And there too was the risen Christ all of a sudden, announcing his presence with the familiar greeting 'Peace be with you'. Thomas' breath must have been taken away. He had demanded proof of the resurrection by sight and by touch, and here was the risen Christ himself meeting his demand 'Put your finger here and see my hands; and put out your hand and place it in my side; do not be faithless but believing.' But Thomas did neither. Instead he gasped 'My Lord and my God', a full-blooded confession of the risen Christ it took the whole Church some time to make. This is the lesson to learn, that when we undergo a spiritual experience of the risen Christ, visible and tangible proof are unnecessary, indeed they are out of place.

Does a question arise here? Why did the Lord offer Thomas a sign to help him to faith which he categorically refused to give the Pharisees in the days of his ministry in Galilee? The answer is simple – because Thomas wanted to believe and couldn't, and the Pharisees couldn't believe because they didn't want to. In matters of belief a start is not even possible for those who do not want to believe.

And so now we see this temperamentally melancholy man rapturous in his faith. What he had always wanted to believe, but dared not risk believing for fear there should be no substance behind it, and his melancholy in consequence driving him down to a living death, had now come to him in the Christian assembly. Did he dance for joy? I doubt it. Melancholy types can't dance. They might even appear comic if they tried. But he was a different man, a far happier man, there was a light in his eye and a lift in his step, and I guess if ever he went to India as tradition says he did (and I don't know), he helped many a man and many a woman to faith in the risen Christ, not least because he was able to testify how once he was in the position of asserting 'I can't take it'. All that changed because he never gave up longing to believe. The risen Christ does not leave such a man without faith. The day comes when it breaks in; in all likelihood it will be when he assembles with believing Christians at worship. 'I can't take it' will be transfigured into 'I do take it'; I believe in the risen Christ.

6. Matter and Spirit

Acts 10.38, 40, 41 (NEB) *You know about Jesus of Nazareth, how . . . God raised him to life on the third day, and allowed him to appear, not to the whole people, but to witnesses whom God had chosen in advance – to us, who ate and drank with him after he rose from the dead.*

Oh dear! – 'ate and drank with him after he rose from the dead'. Did you hear that? Did Cornelius, the Roman army captain, his relations and friends gathered together in his house at Caesarea down by the sea, blink when they heard these words drip off St Peter's lips, 'ate and drank with him after he rose from the dead'? Or were they such simple folk they did not bother their heads about such complicated questions as the relationship between the spiritual and the material? We certainly blink, and probably swallow hard. How could the risen Christ with that spiritual body of his, so other than material and physical that he could appear and disappear at will, how could he partake of material sustenance?

1. An awkward story

We want to bypass this story as that other story also by the same author, St Luke, in his gospel. We read how in the evening of Easter Day the assembled disciples were 'startled and terrified' to find Jesus standing among them. 'They thought they were seeing a ghost.' Who wouldn't? But he reproved them. Why your questionings? he said; 'Look at my hands and feet. It is I myself. Touch me and see; no ghost has flesh and bones as you can see I have.' They were still unconvinced. So he asked them, 'Have you anything here to eat?' They offered him a piece of fish they had cooked, which he took and ate before their eyes. (Luke 24.36–43).

Is this where we 'switch off'? If we do, let us not do so before we attempt to hear what this strange passage of

30

scripture may be saying by the way it is structured and set in context. It is preceded by the story of the two on the road to Emmaus suddenly accompanied by a third whom they recognized to be the risen Christ, noting the familiar way in which he broke bread at their evening meal. But did this risen figure actually eat the bread? Did he vanish before he had partaken of it? Well, read the account in Luke 24.30, 31. So were they after all encountering a ghost, a disembodied spirit? Is this how the resurrected Jesus is to be understood?

It looks as if this is how the Eleven and the rest of the company thought, even after they heard the story of the two hotly returned from Emmaus. It was a ghost they had seen. And nothing they knew, or did not know, about an empty tomb on Easter morning was sufficient to correct this interpretation. The risen Jesus was a disembodied spirit. Anything like a body, certainly any material frame, had been discarded for ever. There was now no more use for it. God has no future for matter. All this thinking is what the risen Christ was at pains to correct. And he did so by a means we might reckon as bizarre, at least as the story goes, for he ate a piece of cooked fish, with the disciples watching.

Was this a conjuring trick? Was it an act of deceit? – he ate food which he did not need. Suppose then we reject the whole incident. We may: many do. If so, we must face losing what St Luke was anxious to tell us, that the risen body of Jesus was different. It was not a resuscitated corpse; it was not a disembodied spirit. It was different from anything so far guessed at or experienced. It was unique, and the uniqueness (to quote St Peter's words to Cornelius, Acts chapter 10) was 'demonstrated to witnesses whom God had chosen in advance'. And was it not a pointer to what our resurrection bodies will be? Not flesh and blood, certainly, they 'cannot inherit the kingdom of God' as St Paul affirmed (1 Corinthians 15.20) but not disembodied spirits either; no, our resurrected bodies will be something new, something not unconnected with our bodies now, a spiritual body the properties of which we cannot now, as creatures of space and time, even guess.

2. *A possible escape?*

As I have already said, we may reject this story as impossible, that is to say, historically: this eating of a piece of cooked fish by the risen Christ in the presence of the disciples could not have taken place. Yet at the same time we may wish to accept the idea it has to convey as to the nature of our resurrection bodies. They will neither be ghosts nor resuscitated corpses. Could we not then free ourselves from our dilemma by asserting that this teaching of the early Church has been cast into the story form, because only so could it be received by simple folk who respond only to concrete pictures and not to theological or philosophical abstractions? And has not this risen Jesus been placed at the centre of the story so that the whole picture can carry weight? I repeat, is it not possible to escape the awkward bondage to historicity while thus accepting the teaching it has to convey?

Some certainly find relief in this way, and I sympathize; but before we escape too confidently along this route there is a question to ask: how did St Luke, how did the early Church come to the conclusion that our resurrection bodies will be different? Was this part of their Jewish inheritance? It does not appear so. Was it a tenet of Greek philosophy? It certainly was not. On the contrary it stands as a distinctively Christian idea. Then how did it originate? What caused it? Well, what causes any new idea to arise? Is there not such a phenomenon as human inspiration? Cannot a thinker be a pioneer in what he thinks? Yes, indeed, but if we follow this path we must understand that the idea of our resurrection bodies being essentially different has no authority beyond that of any other teaching about life after death; it does not carry the authority of Christ; it cannot be placed in the category of revelation.

3. *A cautious approach*

So I take this strange story seriously. I cannot explain it, I do not profess wholly to understand it, but I am not prepared to

jettison it as stupid or naive. Of course, it seems grotesque for the resurrection body of Jesus to be consuming a piece of cooked fish, but do we really understand what is the relationship of matter and spirit, or indeed of body and mind? What *is* matter anyway? Is it the solid, hard substance most people take for granted? Ask the modern physicist: this is not the answer that will be supplied. Ask a philosopher ancient or modern. And what is the thought that lies behind the Roman Catholic doctrine of Transubstantiation? We may reject the logic as it has been presented, and if we are Protestants we certainly will, but we shall exhibit ourselves as stupid if we reject it out of hand as *obviously* stupid – nothing is obvious when it comes to a consideration of the mystery of existence. To set matter and spirit over against each other as ultimate opposites cannot be right. Furthermore, what is the nature of *transformed* or *transfigured* matter? So had we not better be humble at least before this particular resurrection story of the risen Christ eating a piece of cooked fish in the presence of his disciples? Certainly, if the story does nothing else it can teach us to reserve judgement of what we do not understand; but I think it can do more than this. It can teach us four important truths:
(1) that the resurrection body of Jesus was neither a resuscitated corpse nor a disembodied spirit.
(2) that we ourselves shall be raised with a resurrection body, a transfigured you and me with the individuality to which our flesh and blood has contributed.
(3) that God does not, and will not, treat the material of this world as mere disposable stuff; he made it; it is his.
(4) that the relationship between material and spirit, body and mind, is far more complex than we are apt to think. We shall be wise therefore to credit St Luke with knowing this. Could it not be that he was sufficiently acquainted with Greek thought (he was an educated Gentile) to be at least aware of the problem of existence? So when he came to write his gospel he did not reject what he had been told about the evening of Easter Day when, with the disciples behind closed doors, the risen Christ ate a piece of cooked fish? And he dared to write

this in his second book – the Acts of the Apostles – 'You know about Jesus of Nazareth, how . . . God raised him to life on the third day, and allowed him to appear, not to the whole people, but to witnesses whom God had chosen in advance – to us who ate and drank with him after he rose from the dead.' What ought we to do but pray this prayer, 'Lord, I believe, help thou mine unbelief'.

7.   The Incognito Risen Christ

John 21.5 (NEB)   . . . *the disciples did not know that it was
Jesus.*

Some time ago I was told the following story about the late
Duke of Windsor. When he was Prince of Wales he was staying
with some friends in Nottinghamshire. Looking round the
stables with the other guests he was paid no particular
attention because the presence of royalty on that occasion had
been kept secret. When, however, one of the grooms had been
chatting with him for a little time about the horses he suddenly
stopped and said, 'Excuse me, Sir, but you really are awfully
like the Prince of Wales'. 'I know', replied the Prince without
batting an eyelid, 'I have often been taken for him' – and the
conversation continued about horses.

1. The unrecognized risen Christ

One of the striking features about the resurrection narratives in
the gospels is the way in which the risen Christ is presented as
incognito, so that even the disciples were puzzled to know if it
were he or not.

(a) There was the occasion when he was standing in the
early morning on the shore of the Lake of Galilee, as recorded
in St John chapter 21, when seven of his disciples in a boat
after a night's fruitless fishing saw him there, but they 'did not
know it was Jesus'. And when he called out to them, 'Friends,
have you caught anything?' they still didn't know. Presumably
they reckoned the stranger was simply a prospective buyer
come to fetch some, if any, of the early morning catch. Nor is
this all. When at the man's bidding they shot the net to
starboard to make a catch resulting in an astonishing haul, they
still weren't sure. And the sight of the same man, when they
reached the shore, tending a charcoal fire with fish laid thereon
and bread provided, checked them from asking, 'Who are

you?' They could not square the idea of the risen Christ appearing in such ordinary circumstances, and preparing their breakfast.

(b) Nor is this the only story of such a kind about the risen Christ. St Luke tells of two disciples walking in the evening of Easter Day to the village of Emmaus, some eight miles distant from Jerusalem, and joined by a stranger. Though he talked penetratingly about the Messiah from Moses and the prophets they still did not recognize the stranger as Jesus. And he remained *incognito* till they saw him break bread at table in the old familiar fashion. Then they knew.

(c) And go back to Easter morning itself, Mary Magdalene in the garden supposed that the man to whom she was confiding her grief at the empty tomb was merely the gardener.

(d) There is more: the disciples all together on the evening of Easter day were not wholly convinced that the man standing in their midst was indeed the risen Christ, till they saw the wound marks of crucifixion in his hands and feet.

This is remarkable. If it is claiming too much to assert that these resurrection stories of Jesus in the gospels are *flat* presentations, they certainly lack entirely the splendour and superlative magnificence we should expect in any account of such a stupendous event as the resurrection of the eternal Son of God from the grave. What we might have looked for would be a grand presentation of God's triumph, the sound of trumpets in celestial halls and thousands upon thousands of angels. But no, we have a risen Christ who looked like a gardener, a dusty traveller on a dusty country road, and a man in the early morning asking for fish and cooking the breakfast on a charcoal fire. One decision we must reach – the resurrection of Jesus was not predictable; nor was the way in which the story was to be told. What does it say therefore? To this now we must address our attention.

2. *Three lessons*

(a) First, I think, the resurrection narratives are presented in this quiet, calm, almost pedestrian fashion because the great, public, faith-shaking event in the life of Jesus was not the resurrection but the ugly tearing apart of his body as an exhibit on an offensive gallows, *and all as the Son of God*. This is theologically unthinkable, but it happened. Who could believe that the divine would succumb to human beastliness? but you cannot rub out the cross of Christ from history. What is more, it has been used all over the world, all down the years, to mark the places where Christians have assembled *for worship*. The cross was where Christ won his mighty victory and Easter is the ingathering of its fruits. So the Easter stories are like the still, surprising morning after the terrifying storms of the previous three days. Easter is calm because it points to a battle already won, and won for us.

(b) Secondly, I think, this difficulty Christ's disciples experienced in recognizing him after his resurrection tells us something about the resurrection bodies we ourselves will inhabit. You will remember that when the disciples saw Jesus they thought it was he but they were not sure. He was the same Jesus, and yet he wasn't the same Jesus *in appearance*, and yet there was a continuity between the two. They knew this because they saw the wound marks on his hands and feet produced by the crucifixion nails. And there was the tone of voice in which the risen Jesus addressed Mary Magdalene in the garden, drawing from her the rapturous cry, 'Rabboni'. The question which forces itself on our minds is this; does this strange *half incognito* Jesus after his rising from the grave have any message for us, or is it merely the embroidery on a resurrection legend? I fail to see how it could be, it is so unexpected. Our life in heaven in the future, and the life of those we love who have died, is fundamentally different from our life now; but we shall know each other there, and not in some vague form of spiritual impersonality.

(c) Thirdly, a message for the present from this text – 'the disciples did not know that it was Jesus'. Why didn't they know? – because they did not expect Christ, if he were risen, to appear in such commonplace circumstances. Let us be honest, nor do we. We reckon that if God be God he must make himself known in striking portents and breathtaking miracles. We imagine that if and when God appears there will be no mistaking him. We think some holy place is the only proper location for a theophany; say a shrine, a cathedral, or at least some religious building with a 'holy man' in attendance. But no, these resurrection narratives give no support for such ideas. The risen Christ appeared in ordinary, commonplace and, if I may risk the word, secular settings.

Is this still true and does this still happen? Does God still make his existence known in unexpected places? Here is a man who rarely goes to church; by no means could he be labelled as a 'religious type', but one evening finds him in the Albert Hall at a 'prom' concert. In the programme is Beethoven's fifth symphony, and somehow the music grips him. The strident passages ring true to his own life – his experience has been very like that. And then there flows over him the great finale in a triumphant C major key. And this man, seated up there in the gallery in the cheap seats, is uplifted. Suddenly there seems to be more to life than Friday's pay packet, he feels another dimension altogether. What is this? It is nothing less than the transcendent breaking into this man's pedestrian circumstances, which he may not recognize because he does not expect God to make himself known to ordinary people like himself, to someone in the cheap seats in the Albert Hall.

Here is a mother hoping against hope that her daughter will come home for Christmas. But the daughter has got mixed up with a 'fast set', and if she makes excuses for not coming the mother will know she has lost her daughter. Desperately she prays, but as soon desists: will the sovereign Lord of the Universe concern himself with her homely case? It is a pity she did not know the lesson of these flat resurrection narratives. The Lord does appear, he does enter into the circumstances of the most ordinary people.

Even the Lord's disciples failed to grasp this at first but they came to recognize in their midst him who was at first *incognito*. And then everything was changed for them. The world looked a different place. There was a light in their eye not seen before, and a spring in their step. The recognition of the risen Christ brings this about; it really does. God comes where we are, and life is never quite the same again.

8. The Thirteenth Witness

1 Corinthians 15.8 (NEB) *In the end he appeared even to me.*

I don't know if I need, but I always feel a little sorry for the twelfth man in a cricket team. He is neither in nor out of the first eleven; he is in fact *almost* in, his name is attached to the eleven, but he may never play. Yet he could play, he is up to the standard required, but being a reserve the opportunity may not arise. In a way he is all trained-up and keyed-up for nothing. There is no report on him after the match. He simply sat throughout in the pavilion.

1. An odd witness

Today I am going to tell you about the thirteenth witness to the risen Christ, but he isn't a bit like the twelfth man attached to a cricket eleven; he is not a reserve, someone who in all probability will not play. On the contrary, he is the most important witness of them all, and for a very special reason which I hope we shall all grasp because it carries an important implication.

Let us at the outset fix the first twelve. They were the twelve disciples of Jesus, often called apostles. One of them, Judas Iscariot, defected and was replaced by Matthias of whom we know nothing except that he attached himself to Jesus from the very beginning of his ministry and never wavered, becoming in the end a witness to his resurrection. Of the other eleven, most Christians will be acquainted with the name of the leading apostle – St Peter, not least because of the great church in Rome, the city where he met his death. James, John and Andrew might be familiar, and possibly Thomas, 'doubting Thomas'. It is unlikely that most of us could complete the list however. And the odd fact is that not even the New Testament writers were absolutely sure, because although there is more

40

than one list of their names they do not exactly tally. But if there was any uncertainty about all the twelve, there was no uncertainty whatsoever about the thirteenth witness. Every Christian knew his name, and so will you when I tell you – St Paul, the name which even eclipses the word 'London' attached to that city's own cathedral – it is St Paul's Cathedral, not London Cathedral. So St Paul dominates the New Testament as a witness to the risen Christ, the thirteenth man even overtops St Peter, the first.

And yet it is odd that St Paul should be a witness; he thought so himself. We have this phrase of his in 1 Corinthians 15.8 'In the end he appeared even to me'. And he goes on to elaborate, 'this birth of mine', that is to say, this spiritual birth of mine, this sudden enlightenment which made me a witness 'was monstrous'. I was like one born out of due time, for, after all, the list of apostles was complete. There were twelve, so I was an odd thirteenth. What St Paul actually wrote about himself in the Greek is startling, *to ektrōma* – 'the abortion'. He explains, 'for I had persecuted the Church of God and was therefore inferior to all other apostles – indeed, not fit to be called an apostle. However, by God's grace I am what I am, nor has his grace been given to me in vain; on the contrary, in my labours I have outdone them all – not I, indeed, but the grace of God working with me.' Thus the thirteenth witness becomes the most prominent witness.

2. Why a witness at all?

But why? You may know that the qualification for being called an apostle was having kept company with Jesus all the while he was coming and going in his ministry from the very beginning until the day he was taken up; the ascension. But Paul had not done this. We don't know whether he ever met Jesus or even saw or heard him. He did not see him arrested, tried and condemned to that terrible crucifixion, he had not fled into hiding when it all happened for fear he should be crucified himself as did all the other apostles; no, he was casting men and women into prison himself, goading them to blaspheme the name of Christ. Nor was Paul by the garden tomb on Easter morning peering in to draw any conclusions that might be possible. He was not in the room with all the apostles gathered when the two travellers burst through the fast closed door with the news 'Christ is risen!' All this time Paul was nursing his loathing and sharpening his hatred of this dangerous sectarian following of Jesus which he feared might gain a hold. So how could Paul be classed an apostle even though there followed his dramatic conversion to Christ on the Damascus Road? Only because he was convinced that the one who appeared to him was the *risen Christ*. He heard this voice calling 'Saul, Saul, why do you persecute me?' And when he cried 'Tell me, Lord, who you are' the voice answered 'I am Jesus whom you are persecuting'. And the genuineness of the experience was confirmed by the subsequent life-long energy-expending and self-sacrificial testimony that marked him out in the Roman empire of his time, a key man in the history of the world.

3. *The significance of the thirteenth witness*

All this is true, but the real significance of St Paul, however, is not the startling nature of his conversion, nor of his becoming an apostle extraordinary, the thirteenth witness; St Paul is pre-eminent because his preaching of the risen Christ makes it possible for us to believe that the story we are told of what Jesus did and said, and what happened to him, is substantially true.

Let me spell this out: it needs spelling out. On any reading, the story of Jesus of Nazareth is unusual to say the least. A carpenter's son, a carpenter himself for many years with work-worn hands, no education beyond a village school, no university training, an upbringing and almost a whole life restricted by provincial Galilee (one of the less significant parts of the Roman Empire, indeed hardly reckoned with at all except as sometimes a political nuisance). And Jesus' ministry there on leaving the carpenter's shop did not last much longer than three years, if that, and was cut short by a form of execution reserved only for the offscouring of society. But covering that short appearance on the public stage were accounts of astonishing works of healing, and utterances the penetrating depth of which has never been surpassed, and to crown it all, confident testimonies to his resurrection from the grave, so that he came to be trusted as Son of God, the Christ, the Messiah, the Saviour of the World. Is all this credible? Frankly it is not credible by the ordinary processes of historical research. No doubt there was a Jesus of Nazareth, one would be as stupid to deny his existence as to go around affirming that there never was an Alexander the Great or a Caesar Augustus. But you cannot prove that he worked miracles, or that he rose from the dead, or that his was a 'virgin birth', or that he was the Son of God. The materials for logical proof simply do not exist.

4. The need for a preacher

So where are we? Out in the uncertain waters of wishful thinking? Relegated to the credulous who will believe anything so long as a sufficient number of people repeat it? Or must we lumber along with an awkward agnosticism which sees the attraction of faith but can't 'get round to it'?

This is where St Paul comes in. He so preached Christ that the lives of men and women netted in a hopeless, even if sophisticated, paganism were turned round to discover meaning in our human existence. They knew in their bones then that Christ was real because through responding to Paul's preaching their own lives had become more real; they had lost their emptiness. Inner peace had replaced inner conflict, hope had taken over from despair, purpose from a prevailing pointlessness. This happened in Syria, it happened in Cyprus, it happened in Asia Minor, it happened in Greek city after

Greek city; it happened in thrusting, cruel Rome. Place was no barrier, culture or lack of it was no barrier, nor did race constitute any kind of blockage. The preaching of Christ evoked faith wherever there was a willingness to hear. And when once faith was alight – please listen to this bit because it contains the nub of all our thought today – when once faith was alight in the human heart, the human mind was ready to accept as substantially true the records we have in the New Testament of Jesus's life and resurrection. Jesus did live like this, he did die like this, and he was raised from the dead like this. Belief in the history of Jesus depends on faith in the preached Christ. The situation is not the other way round. We cannot have proof first and then hope to have faith. The materials are not available.

Why was there a thirteenth witness? Why were not the twelve sufficient? Because there was a desperate need for a preacher if the story of Jesus on which our salvation hinges was to be believed. Eternal life depends on what happened, it is wrapped up in what Jesus actually did. But a preacher needs education and skill; a great preacher needs a great deal of education and skill. A fisherman from Galilee, though St Peter did wonders, is scarcely capable, and a tax-collector would not be up to it. If the story of Jesus was to be believed and that offensive gallows scene at Calvary explained, an intellectual giant was essential. That giant was St Paul, the thirteenth witness. It is *because of the thirteenth witness* that there exists the story of Jesus to believe in today.

9. The Christian Facts

1 Corinthians 15.3 (NEB) *First and foremost, I handed on to you the facts which have been imparted to me.*

I wonder if there are any photographs or paintings of faces to which you are able to go back again and again for the sheer pleasure of looking at them. For me there are at least two. The face of John Keble, a leader of the Oxford Movement and author of many well-known hymns; and also the face of Edith Cavell whom the Germans in the early morning of 5 August 1915 led out to the stake, blindfolded and shot: it was because she, a British nurse, had helped British soldiers caught in the rapid German advance into Belgium to escape. I know tastes in faces differ, as in many other departments of life – *chacun à son goût* – but for me these two faces are of surpassing beauty. And I have to ask myself, suppose it were possible for me to meet someone who had known them personally, what would we talk about? Certainly not the weather! I should ask, what was he really like? What sort of person was she in ordinary life? Tell me more, I feel I must know the facts.

There came a day when St Paul went up to Jerusalem with the express purpose of seeing St Peter. No, not simply to find out what he looked like. The Greek word in Galatians 1.18 where he tells us about this visit is very strong – *historēsai*. It means 'to enquire', to visit for the sake of discovering what needs to be known; like making a journey to a medical specialist in Harley Street in London. St Paul was desperate to find out the facts about Jesus of Nazareth. And what better source of information than St Peter who knew him personally and intimately, and was his chiefest disciple? Both these men, St Peter and St Paul, had experienced the risen Christ individually, both of them had publicly repudiated Jesus, and both of them were completely transformed characters on account of what had happened to them. Strong men they were, thrusting and integrated, liable to clash.

And they were together for a fortnight. What did they talk

about? The state of the national economy? St Paul, you can be certain, pressed St Peter – what was Jesus of Nazareth really like? What was his attitude to the Jewish law? Did he really forgive the woman taken in adultery? Did he expect his life would end shamefully on a public gibbet? Was he actually buried? Was he raised up on the third day? Did you see him thereafter, Peter, you yourself? And what about the Twelve? Were there any others outside this inner circle who saw him after his resurrection? Tell me Peter! I must know the facts. I have been in Arabia for three years since my conversion, thinking, thinking, thinking. What is more I feel constrained, now chosen by God, to preach the gospel of the risen Christ who I too have seen, but I *cannot* unless I know the facts about Jesus as the Church has received them. Tell me, Peter, what happened.

1. The necessity for the Christian facts

I think the first point to notice in all this is that if the risen Christ is to be preached, personal experience of him is not enough, there has to be acceptance of certain historical facts handed down; what the New Testament calls the *paradosis*, or deposit; otherwise the Christian faith could be, in essence, someone's 'bright idea'.

Not that the personal experience is dispensable; it is necessary for the whole Church in order to give it life, and it is especially necessary for the preacher. Not that it must be of the Damascus road type. Most of us have never known anything of a blinding flash such as St Paul (or Saul of Tarsus as he was then called) experienced, with a voice calling, 'Saul, Saul why are you persecuting me. I am Jesus whom you are persecuting'. No, but Christ is much more for us than a name in a history book, or a theological manual. He is one of whom we rejoice to confess, 'He loved me and gave himself up for me'. This is a self-authenticating testimony. It needs no proof. Ask any mystic, he will not dither about its genuineness. Even so, personal, mystical, interior religious experience is not enough. There has to be content with certain basic historical facts, though it be second-hand, otherwise our faith has no roots; and if it has no roots then the time will come when it has no fruits. Uprooted faith dies. Cut if off from the resurrection of Jesus and there is no risen Christ in it. Then the preaching is powerless, it converts no one, it scarcely even reforms.

Knowing all this and more St Paul went up to Jerusalem to see St Peter with the urgent plea – tell me more about Jesus of Nazareth and what actually happened. I must know the facts.

2. The necessity for the Church

A second point for us to grasp is that our faith has to line up with the faith of the whole body of believers, called the Christian Church. We have to belong to the believing Church.

Now, St Peter at Jerusalem was the representative of the whole Church; here was another reason why St Paul went to see him. St Paul very quickly sensed the importance of being connected, indeed being a member of the Church. In the course of time he described the Church as the body of Christ, the mystical body, so that to be incorporated into it is to be incorporated into him, a doctrine which of course makes no sense if Christ is not risen. Certainly this is profound, even difficult teaching, but this we can all grasp, and must grasp, that for all the vividness and authenticity of his personal religious experience, St Paul knew he could not strike out *in isolation* to proclaim the risen Christ, he could only do so in fellowship with the whole Church. He must be accepted; he must belong. So he visited St Peter.

And somebody in the congregation wants to stand up and ask why. Why must the individual believer today belong to the Church? Because the Church is that which carries the faith down the course of history from age to age. You have the faith, I have the faith now, because the Church has not failed to pass it on, well at times, at other times badly, but *it has handed it on.*

The Church is the permanent transmitter. It is also the great reservoir of Christian experience. In it are to be found all types of encounter with the risen Christ, made in all manner of different situations, all manner of cultural settings, all manner of different times and seasons. None of us can ever know the fullness of Christ. At best we can do no more than experience what touching his garment is like. It takes the whole Church together, 'a great multitude which no man can number of every tribe, kindred and tongue' to tell what the risen Christ is for mankind. I must add my testimony, you must add your testimony, but on their own they are not enough, for they are partial. Rightly understood, this is what the Catholic Church is – the whole body of believers containing in its giant reservoir your experience and mine, and a million million others as well. You must belong. I must belong. St Paul knew he had to belong. So he went to see St Peter.

3. The necessity for identification

Thirdly, the Christian needs the Church because he needs a visible organization with which he can identify. Look at the matter this way. Here is a sprawling mass of urban houses. All the buildings are more or less the same. all the gardens are more or less uniform, the streets all look much alike; it is difficult to know one from another. People tell you this is a Christian town, but how do you know? Granted there may be Christian faith in the hearts of some of the residents, but you can't see inside their hearts. But suppose you observe a Church building in the place, a modest building maybe, with only a prefabricated Church spire, but the significant fact is you *can see it*. Something exists with which the residents can identify. There is a Christian identification mark. And that makes all the difference.

Christian baptism functions in this way. It is true that many parents who bring their babies for baptism understand very little of what they are doing, and what baptism really means.

Would to God they knew more! Would to God we clergy could teach them more effectively! But at least they come. They want to identify. Take that opportunity away and what have they left? Take it away and what is there for simple people who never will have a mental grasp of what baptism involves?

I am saying that we need a visible organization with which people can identify, especially if they are inarticulate, to show they have a Christian faith. We need church buildings, we need the sacraments – visible signs of our invisible faith; we need clergy who are seen to be clergy in the street, we need congregations to which we can belong. And it all rests on certain facts – 'Christ died for our sins according to the scriptures, that he was buried, that he was raised to life on the third day according to the scriptures, that he appeared to Cephas (Peter) and afterward to the Twelve. Then he appeared to over five hundred brethren at once.' These are the facts that were handed on to St Paul and which he handed on to the church in Corinth and the other cities he visited. And the heart of them all is this one great fact, 'Christ is risen'. This provides the gospel the Church has to preach. Herein lies our hope, not only for the Church, but for all mankind. For their sakes, for all our sakes, do not lose touch with the Christian facts. Everything hangs on them.

10. Resurrection Titles

Acts 2.36 *Therefore let all the house of Israel know assuredly, that God hath made that same Jesus, whom ye have crucified, both Lord and Christ.*

Some years ago I was taking part in a small committee meeting trying to decide how to allocate certain monies that had been left by a Hebrew Christian, a clergyman. His wish was to provide a scholarship at a certain theological college for some prospective ordination candidate of Jewish origin. It was not an easy task. There were four of us deliberating on this; a bishop, the principal of the theological college, a clerk representing the bank where the capital was deposited, and myself. We got off to a somewhat awkward start because the bank clerk, obviously nervous, did not know how to address the bishop (who was the chairman), and said so. 'Bishop, how do I address you?' The bishop, for his part, had no wish to appear pompous and so replied, 'O call me anything, call me Bill'. But it didn't help; the bank clerk did not address the bishop as Bill, he in fact felt more awkward than ever. So I had stamped on my mind what I already half knew, that titles, like the rules of etiquette, are designed to facilitate social intercourse and not hinder it. Our little committee would have proceeded much more smoothly if the chairman had simply said to the bank clerk, 'Call me bishop.'

Some people are bitterly opposed to titles while others revel in them; they cannot wait to see the honours lists every half year in our newspapers. Both views represent extremes. No doubt there is an improper use of titles, but there is also a proper use. It is as well that we grasp this balance because Jesus was given titles – St Peter made this clear in his sermon on the day of Pentecost; 'Therefore let all the house of Israel know assuredly, that God hath made that same Jesus, whom ye have crucified, both Lord and Christ.' 'Lord' and 'Christ' are titles, and they were given to Jesus after his resurrection and because of his resurrection.

1. Respect

But what did people call Jesus before his resurrection? What did they call him when they saw him walking about in Capernaum, or by the lake of Galilee or striding across the hills between the lake and the sea? There can be no doubt, they called him simply Jesus of Nazareth, adding the 'of Nazareth' because 'Jesus' was a fairly common name. A parallel in our day might be Smith of York of Jones of Cardiff.

After a time, however, they felt awkward. They realized how ahead of them he was intellectually and practically. Not only was his knowledge of the scriptures so profound that the learned Rabbis were no match for him, but he could read people almost at a glance. And his powers of healing were quite extraordinary. Everywhere astonishment followed him. How then could people continue simply calling him Jesus of Nazareth? And so it came about that his disciples called him 'Teacher' or 'Master', and even others who encountered him instinctively addressed him as 'Sir'. Thus the Roman centurion beseeching him for healing on behalf of his slave boy, the Syro-Phoenician mother on behalf of her epileptic daughter, and the Samaritan woman at the well who had never met him before; they felt they had to give him a title of respect. There was nothing official about it. It was entirely voluntary, entirely spontaneous.

How then do we react to Jesus of Nazareth? I doubt if I should be far wrong if I asserted that even in our modern secularized world Jesus receives respect. There is a widespread recognition that he was a remarkable figure. And even if all the miracle stories in the gospels are deleted on the grounds that they are legendary accretions, Jesus still stands out as a sublime teacher; and not only that, but a shining example of what a man could be. But can we go no further? Can we accord him no other titles than simply one which shows him due respect like a pupil calling his teacher 'Sir'?

2. Jesus is Lord

If you wanted to be known as a Christian in the very early days of the Christian Church, long before there was a structured hierarchy, a precise theology or carefully worded creeds, you had to make this confession, 'Jesus is Lord'. This at least was required for baptism. Jesus had to be given the title 'Lord' with all the overtones of divinity that that word conveyed. It was a very bold declaration. Do not forget Jesus had been hanged on a public gallows by the express decree of the Roman power occupying Judaea at the time. He was a disgraced figure, a disowned citizen, a reject from all levels of decent society. Crucifixion was reserved for what would be called in modern times 'the scum of the earth'. They were evil-doers of the lowest class that went to the cross; rebels, criminals, slaves and men of violence. It was too undignified a death penalty to be used on Romans. And here in the Roman empire, in place after place, men and women were prepared to stand up and confess 'Jesus is Lord'. It was a very bold declaration inviting scorn and ridicule if not something worse. It is not difficult to imagine some patrician in Imperial Rome bursting his sides with laughter at the very idea of granting a title to a crucified carpenter: 'My Lord Jesus'.

Nowadays, when what we believe about Jesus is inclined to be fudged even in some church circles, there might be value in calling us again to make the declaration 'Jesus is Lord'. There could hardly be a concentration of three words with more overtones, undertones and implications. Put the accent on the first word, Jesus, and you are rejecting the notion that the Lord we worship is not indentical with the Man of Galilee. Put the accent on the last word, Lord, and you are saying that he partakes of the power and authority of God himself. Put the accent on the middle word, 'is', and you are admitting that

Jesus is alive now which would not be the case if you said Jesus *was* Lord. So you are committing yourself to a belief in the resurrection.

Who then shall say that titles are of no consequence when it comes to our faith in Jesus?

3. *Jesus is the Christ*

And so we return to our text Acts 2.36, 'Let all Israel then accept as certain that God has made this Jesus whom you crucified, both Lord and Messiah.'

This declaration of Jesus' two titles was made in a sermon, and those who heard it did not sleep through it. What is more, when the preacher, the apostle Peter, reached this peroration, they felt as if something had hit them. The narrative says 'When they heard this they were cut to the heart, and said to Peter and to the apostles, "Friends, what are we to do?" '

What was the trouble? The trouble was that for one year, two years, perhaps three years, these same people had been debating whether Jesus was the Christ or not, and had finally reached a negative conclusion. The argument started way back in his predecessor's time. So struck were the priests and Levites with John the Baptist that they asked him if he were 'the Christ', but he flatly denied it. When, however, Jesus came on the scene people wondered, saying, 'When the Christ comes is it likely that he will perform more signs than this man?' And their mutterings grew so persistent that there was a split among them right down the middle, some for, some against. And the authorities, fearing this, sought to end it all by sending the temple police to arrest Jesus, but they did not succeed. So they continued to goad him; 'If you are the Christ tell us plainly'. But they had made up their minds, so much so that if anyone were discovered confessing the Messiahship of Jesus – and the word Christ means Messiah – he would be excommunicated forthwith. And to be excommunicated in that society was to be as good as dead.

Such was the tension; and here now is St Peter standing up in Jerusalem before these same people with this strong proclamation on his lips: 'Therefore let all the house of Israel know assuredly, that God hath made this same Jesus, whom ye have crucified, both Lord and Christ.' *God* has made Jesus Messiah (that is Christ). No matter what you say, think, or have decided, *God has acted*. There is no more to be said. And if you ask, 'But how? when? where?' St Peter will give the same answer, even if you ask a thousand times. Well, look at the resurrection! That God raised Jesus from the dead is the public proclamation of God setting his seal of recognition that Jesus is, what indeed he always was (though hidden), namely both Lord and Christ. They were wrong who in the days of his flesh denied it, they were right who had the faith and the courage to confess it.

So the resurrection on Easter Day is first of all a proclamation about Jesus. He is both Lord and Christ. If we distance ourselves from him, if we respect him but wish to go no further, we may be willing to address him as Jesus of Nazareth, possibly with thoughts of 'Sir' in our minds as to a famous teacher. If, however, we believe in his resurrection we shall have no option but to accord him two titles, Lord and Messiah (or Christ). This puts us in the category of 'Christian', uniting us with all those who make the same confession. The resurrection of Jesus is as decisive as that. We cannot really be Christians if we cut out Easter.

11.   There Must be Witnesses

Acts 1.22 (NEB)   *One of those must now join us as a witness to his resurrection.*

One morning, a few years ago, my wife was driving home from her weekly shopping in Chelsea through Pelham Street in South Kensington. Now Pelham Street is very narrow, so when another car shot out of Pelham Place, a side street, no chance was left for her to avoid a collision. She took the full impact of its bonnet on her offside. Shaken, but not badly hurt, she extricated herself through the nearside door when, to her surprise, a stranger came running up. 'I saw it happen,' he said, 'and it wasn't your fault, the other driver didn't even stop to look before leaving the side street. You can quote me as a witness. Here is my name and address.' And he wrote it down on a piece of paper. What a relief! In settling claims in cases of road accidents one driver's word is as good as another *unless there are witnesses*, though there is the nature of the damage done. But a witness there needs to be, a qualified witness, a witness who can say what he himself saw, not what he heard someone else say he saw.

So it was with the beginnings of the Christian Church (and in a way still is). There had to be witnesses, witnesses of Christ's resurrection, otherwise the Church has no claim to be heard, its preaching is without substance. The eleven apostles were those witnesses, but they had to be *qualified* witnesses, and what the qualifications had to be were spelled out when they set about filling the gap in their number brought about by the defection of Judas.

1. The qualification required

This is what happened. About one hundred and twenty of Jesus' followers assembled in Jerusalem in the wake of an ugly incident. Judas' body had been found in the nearby potter's

55

field. It was to fill the vacancy caused by his death that the qualifications for a prospective candidate came to be spelled out. A member of the apostolic band had to be one who had been in the company of Jesus from the start of his ministry knowing him face to face, and one who also could give his witness that he himself had encountered this same Jesus after he had been crucified, dead and buried, that is in the same company with the other apostles.

There were two men with these unimpeachable qualifications, Joseph and Matthias. Who should it be? How fill the vacancy? Apparently the one hundred and twenty assembled together, prayed and then drew lots. Matthias 'got in', as we say, the second name on the short list; and he, judging from the fact that he does not seem to have been given a popular name like the first candidate, may not have been the favourite. But this only makes the strong point stronger. Nothing about the candidate mattered so much as that he could stand up as a witness to the resurrection of Jesus. Education – lack of education; eloquence – lack of eloquence; pedigree – lack of pedigree; an easy temperament – an awkward temperament; – nothing was the absolute qualification except this, that he had himself encountered the risen Christ, that he was a first-hand witness.

2. A witness implies an event

We are familiar with this necessity to have a first-hand witness in a number of situations. There are the courts of law where counsels for the prosecution and for the defence produce their witnesses. There are reports of desperate famine conditions in the Sudan to which responsible leaders are sent from the affluent countries to witness for themselves the plight of the inhabitants. A dissident is released from a slave labour camp who thereafter becomes a witness to the misery of the thousands still detained. And who has not seen a police notice by the roadside reporting a serious road accident and calling for any who may have witnessed what took place to come forward?

We are familiar, I say, with the indispensable and unique part witnesses play in several important areas of life, but this is what I invite you to notice – a witness implies an event: it implies that something has happened in the external world, something which could either be seen, heard, smelt, touched or tasted. A witness is concerned with the evidence of his senses. He is not asked why something happened as it did, only that it happened. His business is not to relate what other people saw, and what they thought about what they saw. His significance is entirely located in his own personal experience. His analysis of the situation, his forecast of the likely outcome, his advice about what action shall be taken in consequence are totally irrelevant. One requirement and one only is required of a witness – what did you see? What did you hear?

Since, then, a witness implies an event – something has happened – it is difficult to settle with a view of the resurrection of Jesus (as some do) which is almost equivalent to what could be said of Karl Marx – 'he being dead yet speaketh' – in other words his *influence* continues in the world after his death. This is the resurrection. Nor is it easy to be content with the explanation that somehow after his crucifixion the apostles experienced a *growing consciousness* of his spiritual presence, and this is the resurrection. Nor with the view that when the apostles began to preach, Christ came alive in the hearts and minds of the hearers, and this is the resurrection. Surely a witness implies *an event*, an event external to the consciousness of the witness, something to which one at least of his senses can testify. So when the apostles determined with respect to Joseph and Matthias that 'one of those must now join us as a witness to his resurrection' (Acts 1.22) they were referring to something which had actually taken place, and which carried the whole weight of the gospel to be preached, indeed if that event could *not* be substantiated by witnesses the whole Christian edifice would have collapsed. There must be witnesses.

58

3. The appearances of the risen Christ

But witness of what? When I began this sermon I spoke of my wife's car accident, and how a stranger came running up to her and said 'I saw it happen; the other driver pulled out of Pelham Place without looking to see if the main road was clear'. But did the apostles, did Matthias, actually see the resurrection of Jesus happen just like this? Had they been standing before his garden tomb on the Saturday night before Easter with a television camera, could they have made a film of his resurrection? The answer is no. No one saw Jesus emerge from his place of burial. No witness to the event actually taking place is available. So does the case break down? It does not break down if it is accepted that the Jesus the apostles encountered after his death and burial was the same Jesus they had lived with from the very beginning of his ministry in Galilee. The appearances of Jesus after his resurrection constitute the first ground for believing in it. Something did take place. The resurrection of Jesus was an event in time. It actually happened.

4. Witnesses today

Can you and I be witnesses of Christ's resurrection? Can the whole Christian Church be a witness to Christ's resurrection? No, not like the apostles. We have not accompanied Jesus of Nazareth from the beginning of his ministry in Galilee and encountered him right up to the time of his ascension. He has not appeared to us as he did to these twelve men. They must stand apart as *unique* witnesses to the resurrection. But we can and do testify to his risen-ness; the whole Church bears witness to the fact that Christ is risen, he is alive. We do not merely commemorate a dead hero, we worship a living Lord with whom we have spiritual fellowship, now.

Some months ago I came across the story of the American Colson who was sent to prison for his part in the Watergate scandal. What he tells is as exciting as any novel. When the sentence of imprisonment was passed, a text from St Paul's letter to the Romans burned in his mind: 'Neither death, nor life, nor angels, nor principalities, nor powers, can separate us from the love of God which is in Christ Jesus.' And it changed him, there in the prison; and before he was discharged he had already formed a prayer group among his fellow prisoners. He had become a witness to the risen-ness of Christ. Maybe this story 'turns you off', as we say. Too emotional! Too dramatic! Not your style! Very well. Here is a drop-out who has found a purpose in life. Here is a marriage grown stale and now renewed. Here is an embittered widow who has discovered that an occasion of offering help to those in need has soothed her sores. There is a great cloud of witnesses of this kind. Look at your 'Songs of Praise' programme on television. Are not these the sort of results you would expect if Christ is not dead, but truly risen and alive?

This is therefore the place to start believing in the resurrection of Christ and the truth of Easter – the experience of people today. Then if we go back to the New Testament and read what it has to say happened, taking note of the witnesses who had a special role to play, we may well cry out, 'Yes, I see'. So will we have a foundation on which to build our own lives, full of hope and meaning? The spiritual world is real. Our future is assured. Our loved ones are not lost in oblivion. Christ is risen, Alleluia. There are witnesses in plenty.

12. The Resurrection Faith

2 Timothy 4.7 (NEB) *I have run the great race, I have finished the course, I have kept faith.*

Not long ago I was invited to preach at a 'Festival of Faith', and after I had agreed there came a second letter giving me my text, 'I have kept faith'. I did as I was told, though smothering a laugh all to myself because had the invitation come from an examiner in New Testament interpretation I should have guessed he was trying to catch me out; because there are traps in this verse for the unwary – what the German theologians call *Frühkatholismus* and all that. But of course the vicar in question was not trying to catch me out, nothing of the kind, though the traps are there; and we shall, I think, understand our faith a little better if we see what they are.

1. St Paul's great race

First look at the setting just as it stands. Here is St Paul with long years of wearisome prison sentence behind him. Much of it had not been harsh maybe, not like the horrible confinement in filthy cells in the vaults below the Colosseum in Rome many a Christian had to endure later on at the hands of Roman cruelty and coarseness; but no freedom, no privacy, no variation, always the dreadful clanking of the chain linking him to a succession of guards responsible for his life. More oppressive still, always the foreboding sentence of death hanging over him coupled with tormenting delays of fixing his trial. But it must come soon. Perhaps tomorrow he will be marched out to a dock. Charges will be laid against him, trumped-up charges; and then the hurried exit and the swift stroke of the executioner's sword; for, being a Roman citizen, that is how they would kill him.

St Paul was getting on in years. His had been a long run and a full life. There had been times of exquisite joy and there had been times of heartbreaking disappointment. He recalled the hostility in Antioch in Pisidia, Iconium and Lystra in the early days of the Gentile mission, and the bloodcurdling cries of the crowds in Jerusalem not so long ago. And all because he had stayed faithful to the gospel of the risen Christ and the proclamation of his name as the Saviour of us all, whatever our race, background, sinfulness or uprightness.

Of course there had been triumphs too. There was Philippi, Corinth and Ephesus; and crowds of friends, friends some of whom so loved him they fell on his neck and kissed him when they saw him make for the ship at Miletus, knowing they would see his face no more. This is always one of the rewards for preaching the gospel; friends who never forget you till their dying day. Luke was one such for St Paul, Timothy another. Paul thought of him especially during his last imprisonment, and of the work entrusted to him in the ministry in the Church.

So there in the prison he called from a writing tablet and dictated some of the material now incorporated in the two letters addressed to Timothy in the New Testament. In the second of them occur the words 'As for me, already my life is being poured out on the altar, and the hour of my departure is upon me. I have run the great race, I have finished the course, *I have kept faith*. And now the prize awaits me, the garland of righteousness which the Lord, the all-just Judge, will award me on that great Day; and it is not for me alone, but for all who have set their hearts on his coming appearance.'

2. *Keeping faith with the gospel*

What could Paul have meant by these words in his letters, 'I have kept faith, and now the prize awaits me, the garland of righteousness which the Lord, the all-just Judge, will award me on that great Day'? Could he possibly have meant, 'I have lived a good life, and so when my time comes to die God will make a favourable assessment of my moral record and in consequence award me the prize of immortality, crowning me with the garland of righteousness I have striven for, just as the runners in the athletic contests in the Greek and Roman cities used to be capped with a wreath of laurel leaves? Is this what Paul meant? But is not this how many people today view the issue of their lives? God will tot up our good behaviour marks and our bad behaviour marks and if the former are in excess of the latter then the reward of eternal life will be ours? But there is no gospel in this; no good news at all for the sinner, the weak man or weak woman, no hope at all for the lost sheep! Surely up and down the length and breadth of the Roman Empire Paul had preached the risen Christ as the Saviour of all who simply turn to him, put themselves on his side, trust him and believe in him; that is, put their faith in him. All our whole future is summed up in the risen Christ. He is our rescuer, our deliverer, our Lord and our King. Paul never deviated from this gospel, not even if he had to argue for it and suffer for it. By faith we are united to Christ who died and rose again, and so shall we die and rise again. Faith then is decision. It is deciding for Christ, it is counting ourselves as his people – and we are then safe. How could Paul be more explicit? how more radical? how more simple? how more broad? This is the gospel with which, throughout the long course of his career now coming to a close, he had 'kept faith'. I am quite sure he would have sung John Newton's hymn had he known it –

> How sweet the name of Jesus sounds
> In a believer's ear!
> It soothes his sorrows, heals his wounds,
> And drives away his fear.

His prize at the last then was not for good conduct, though his conduct had been consistently good; it was for being faithful to the gospel of our salvation by grace through faith in the risen Christ.

3. The Faith

This is all true, quite true, but is the New English Bible right to translate what Paul wrote as 'I have kept faith'? The Greek is 'I have kept *the faith*'. This is how the Authorized Version, the Revised Version, the Revised Standard Version and the Jerusalem Bible all translate it. Most of us have been brought up on this rendering, and I have to say it is correct. Here faith is represented as a body of beliefs, almost a set of doctrines, something rather like the Apostles' Creed; all very different from simple trust in a person as when Jesus said to the woman with a haemorrhage, 'My daughter, your faith has cured you. Go in peace, free for ever from this trouble' (Mark 5.34 (NEB). This is primary and fundamental faith. But can we dispense with doctrines at some stage? Suppose some preacher begins asserting that Jesus never died on the cross but only swooned! Does this matter? Or that he did not rise from the dead; what the disciples experienced was an internal spiritual encounter? Suppose it is said that Jesus was not in a unique sense Son of God but only a very good man like the saints only better, what then becomes of our simple faith in Christ as the Saviour? And this was the trouble when this second letter to Timothy in the New Testament was compiled incorporating some of St Paul's own words. False teachers were travelling around the young churches causing hundreds to lose their faith because the stones in the foundation of it were being prized out. So it does matter *what* we believe as well as *in whom* we believe. Surely, if the resurrection of Christ goes, if he is not the risen Christ, everything goes. Our faith is empty.

So the creeds we recite in church are important, not as doctrinal tablets to be swallowed whole with a gulp in order that we may attain to the life eternal, nor as fences outside which there is no salvation at all. They are guide-lines rather like those red and white plastic cones the police place in the roadway to keep the traffic in the safety path. We can so easily lose our faith; and therefore guide-lines concerning what we believe *about* Christ are important in order to safeguard our simple faith *in him* as the risen Christ. His name means everything.

Let me end with a story. It is told by one called Rudolf Bösinger, a German soldier in the last war. Severely wounded on the Russian Front, he lay with a number of the wounded, weak with dysentry, in a church not far from Moscow. In the half light he suddenly realized that a man was standing over him demanding his name; a Russian. In his weakened, half-delirious state, however, he could not bring it to mind. Such blank forgetfulness terrified him. He thought he must be going mad. Then a name did involuntarily float into his mind. It was like a shaft of wonderful sunlight, and he said it out loud, the name in which he had trusted all his life – 'Christus, Christus, Christus' (the German for Christ). 'No, No, No' shouted the Russian official, 'you . . . fool. I want *your* name.' But the half-dead, half-alive German could say no more. For his part there was no need to say any more. The groaning and the stench all around him in the chapel faded out; he was at peace. The name of Christ was all he needed for what he thought was to be his final passage out beyond the world.

> How sweet the name of Jesus sounds
> In a believer's ear!
> It soothes his sorrows, heals his wounds,
> And drives away his fear.
>
> It makes the wounded spirit whole,
> And calms the troubled breast;
> 'Tis manna to the hungry soul,
> And to the weary rest.

Such simple faith in Christ is the heart of the matter. St Paul kept to that. 'I have kept faith.' I have kept *the* faith, because that is what it is.

13. Resurrection Life-style

Colossians 3.1 (RSV) *If you have been raised with Christ,
seek the things that are above, where Christ is, seated at the
right hand of God.*

Some time ago I heard a story which ran something like this (I
am not sure if it is true or not but it could well have been). It
was about a village lad who joined the navy. No one knew him
as a particularly tidy young man, indeed he was scarcely ever
seen in any other clothes but grubby slacks and a moth-eaten
sweater. The day came, however, when he returned from the
navy's recruitment centre smartly turned out in a complete
sailor's uniform. He was hardly recognizable. The village 'yob'
was not a sailor. He looked like a sailor. His mother was proud
of him and the girls in the village turned to look at him, for
every girl loves a sailor it is said. But was he really a sailor?
What did he know even about the most elementary nautics?
His father, a wise man, sensed the boy's inner uncertainty and
had a talk with him; this is what he said: 'Son, you are a sailor
now, you are wearing the uniform, now it is up to you to *be
what you are.*'

1. Status and achievement

'Now it is up to you to be what you are.' The same could be
said to every baptized Christian, and certainly to every baptized and confirmed Christian – 'Be what you are'. All who
have thus put on Christ's uniform are in his service, and the
wearing of the uniform carries with it responsibilities about
life-style. I once heard of a bishop who made this point the
subject of every confirmation address. The pity was he had no
idea of how mystified the candidates were, especially the
younger ones, to be informed that they had 'put on the livery
of the Lord'. Some had their work cut out to suppress their
giggles. But his aim was right. The confirmed are to be what
they are.

It is the relationship between status and achievement which is at stake here. Which of the two comes first? Do we say to a young medical student, 'You must achieve success first as a medical practitioner with years of experience behind you, before we call you a doctor?' or do we call him a doctor straight away after qualifying, believing that this new status will call forth his achievement? In other words he will become what he is, his status will contribute to his achievement.

So it is then in the Christian ordering of life. A man, a woman, even a child sufficiently old enough to understand something of the faith and who believes, is counted a Christian, and properly counted a Christian, long before he/she exhibits all the Christian virtues or even half of them. What is involved here is the frequently misunderstood, and frequently maligned doctrine, of justification by faith. How can any individual be accounted good (not to use the proper word 'righteous') if he is a long way from being thoroughly good? Does this mean behaviour and life-style do not matter? So long as we say 'we believe' and, so far as we can and do actually believe, we are all right? – Surely this is immoral? No, it is not immoral. The call to the Christian believer is – Yes, you are a Christian by faith in Christ, then be what you are! Live up to your uniform.

Now we are in a position to grasp the force of St Paul's urge to the Christians in Colossae, 'If you have been raised with Christ, seek the things that are above, where Christ is, seated at the right hand of God'. If you have been raised! Only you can know if you are on Christ's side, only you can decide for him, that is put your faith in him – then of course you are raised with him; be what you are then – a Christ-raised person!

2. What has to go

Maybe we take this 'lying down'. There is little to disturb us here, or so we reckon. After all what can the practical meaning be of St Paul's injunction 'seek the things that are above, where

Christ is, seated at the right hand of God'. This kind of vague spiritual language is all very well, we complain, for people of a mystical bent, but some of us are engineers, gardeners, laboratory technicians, nurses, computer technicians. We deal all day with material objects that have to be seen, touched and manipulated. What use is it telling us to 'set our minds on things that are above, not on things that are on the earth'? Where should we be in our modern competitive world if we moved dreamily about with our 'heads in the clouds', which seems to be what the apostle is commending here? Surely, when the New Testament brings this kind of language before us, it is time politely but firmly to bid it 'Good afternoon', and be gone!

Then before you know where you are, St Paul 'puts his boot in'. And now I am going back to the Prayer Book version of this New Testament reading. I am doing so because for years and years this is what all clergymen who have been in the ministry as long as I, had to read on Easter Day to congregations that were the most numerous of the whole year. There was no choice. It really was like 'putting the boot in'. There we were going along so smoothly, so aesthetically, with daffodils and lilies all around us when suddenly we bumped down from our lovely spirituality into blatant realism. Did it jar? Of course it jarred. I guess it was meant to jar. There is to be no fudging where we are to start as raised-with-Christ Christians – 'Mortify therefore your members which are upon the earth; fornication, uncleanness, inordinate affection (RSV passion), evil concupiscence (RSV evil desire), and covetousness, which is idolatry: for which things' sake the wrath of God cometh on the children of disobedience.' And just when we had begun to settle down again (did the priest pause before he uttered the last sentence in order to heighten the impact? only if he was a brave man) 'in the which ye also walked some time, when ye lived in them'.

So permissiveness has to go; and dirty-mindedness has to go; and seeing women as essentially sex objects, and pornography, and scheming to seduce the other man, the other woman; and wife swapping; and strip clubs; and sleeping around; and the whole sex industry racket that is filling unscrupulous pockets. Of course it will continue in the world. It was rife in Colossae and in all the Greek cities where St Paul had established churches and to which he addressed letters now incorporated in the New Testament. What is more, the church members, before they became Church members, had been mixed up in such ways of life. 'But', said St Paul, in effect, 'all that represents the pagan way of life and you must have none of it. *Be what you are*, risen-with-Christ Christians. Yours must be a different life style.'

3. We do have to pay

Does this sound tough? But this scripture passage, this Easter Day epistle which should be read in the ASB and not only in the BCP, hasn't finished. Commenting on the pagan life-style which is both ancient and modern, flourishing in the affluent West no less than in the deprived East, it adds, 'On account of these the wrath of God is coming'. As much as to say, 'Don't kid yourselves.' You think the Christian life-style is an optional extra, a kind of icing on the cake which a few narrow-minded people fancy is attractive; all right, maybe for monks, nuns and celibates (if even they can take it), but not for ordinary full-blooded men and women: but don't kid yourselves, those who do not seek the Christian life-style as opposed to the pagan run a terrible risk. As the last war slogan had it on the posters in the London Underground and other public places warning against venereal disease – 'Clean living is the only safeguard'. That warning would seem to be even more apposite today and of wide application.

I haven't enjoyed preaching this sermon. Everything about me constrains me to dodge its awful direction. I derive no satisfaction whatsoever from seeing men and women, and particularly young men and women completely outside the church and the sphere of its influence, let alone those inside it, make a mess of their lives. I am not so spiritually-minded as not even to know what fleshly-mindedness is. But I can see a day coming, if it has not come already, when a fallen world is going to point a finger of accusation at the church for soft-pedalling the judgement theme which goes alongside the mercy theme in the proclamation of the gospel. There are laws which govern healthy living which is one of the meanings of the Bible's word 'salvation'; and if we reckon there are none, or that we can ignore them, we shall pay, and pay now in this life. It looks as if we are paying already.

4. Attractive performance

Before I finish, let me lift our eyes to something more attractive. To me one of the most beautiful sights is an Olympic runner, say in the thousand metre race, pulling away from the others as he comes in sight of the winning post. Those long strides, that perfect rhythm; arms, legs, the whole body working in harmonious cooperation, almost like a well-tuned machine. That is how the risen-with-Christ life-style should be; if not physically, certainly as regards character and mastery of life. 'If you have been raised with Christ, seek the things that are above, where Christ is, seated at the right hand of God.' Be what you are. This I can promise you, you will enjoy running along like that.

14.   Knowing the Risen Christ

Hebrews 13.8   *Jesus Christ is the same yesterday, today and for ever.*

There are some verses in the Bible which do not rely on their context for the light with which they shine, although they may be offset by it. Hebrews 13.8 is such a one; 'Jesus Christ is the same yesterday, today and for ever'. This text, and those like it, strike one as does some outstanding flowering shrub in a garden, say an azalea, so conspicuous for its mass of flaming red that the eyes cannot move away from it, especially in the evening sunlight which somehow makes the colour even more dazzling. All the beauty is in the plant. It would command attention even if it grew in someone's back garden in a suburb and not in the botanical gardens at Wisley. It is gazed at, and gazed at again, perhaps even photographed so that its amazing beauty may be drawn on in the dark days of winter.

1. Dependable

Hebrews 13.8 is like that plant; 'Jesus Christ is the same yesterday, today and for ever'. Everything is concentrated here on one name, one figure, one man – Jesus Christ. We are not encouraged to wander around and look where we will, only at him; and above all at this one attribute, that he is always the same; 'Jesus Christ is the same yesterday, today and for ever'.

It is not difficult to think of some ordinary person of whom it could be said, 'You know, old So-and-So is always the same, that is the good thing about him'. He could be an employer, an official at the tax office, or the greengrocer at the corner shop (if there is one left). The outstanding merit of this man is that he is not cheerful one day and grumpy the next, not helpful one day and a stone wall the day after. But with a man who is you never know why. That is the trouble. Is it his liver out of sorts? Did he just get out of bed the wrong side that morning? Whatever the reason he is not dependable. You never know

70

what will be the outcome of your visit to him. It could be beneficial; it could be a set-back. All in all is it not true that we give high praise to the man or woman of whom we can say, 'he/she is always the same'? It is possible to do business with people who are dependable.

Is this a commonplace, almost trite, an analogy for what this outstanding text says of Jesus Christ? Whether trite or not it is important that we grasp this truth when we come to consider the *risen* Christ. Though unrestricted now as a spiritual presence he is the same as he was in Galilee and Judaea, the same as when he reacted to the widow woman bereaved of her only son, the same as when the Roman army captain appealed on behalf of his servant boy, the same as when the crowds jostled him grasping at his healing powers. The risen Christ is not superior in essence to the incarnate Christ. As people in need, or indeed in hostility, approached him in Galilee and Judaea so we can now. He is the same Christ. He will respond now as he responded then and so he will tomorrow. There will be the same compassion, the same forgiveness and the same strong call to sacrifice for what is right and good and true.

A friend of mine was telling me the other day of how one with whom she worked on close terms got promotion to what would have to be reckoned a somewhat glamorous position. The friendly association dropped after the promotion. A gap opened up; there was no more coming and going. The promoted one, mixing now in higher circles (so-called) dropped her one-time friend. She had not remained the same. Experiences of let-down like that hurt.

My text for today provides the assurance that the risen Christ does not let us down. He is always the same, the same in character as he was as the man of Galilee, the man who lived for others even if they were outsiders – especially if they were outsiders.

2. Knowable

But what was Jesus like as the man of Galilee? This is not

merely a matter of interest or historical enquiry. It is important for our spiritual life now. To know the risen Christ we must know the incarnate Christ. Unless the statement 'Jesus Christ is the same yesterday, today and for ever' is to remain only as a pious clichè empty of real content, there must be a story of Jesus to tell. And there is. It is presented in the writings of the four evangelists (as they are called), Matthew, Mark, Luke and John. I am well aware that two or three years ago on the television at tremendous expense, and with almost total disregard of the general unanimity of most New Testament scholars, doubt was cast on the historical reliability of these documents. We can however be sure that, given questionable points here and there, we have in the New Testament a substantially reliable picture of the man Jesus, and even some of the actual words he spoke, *ipsissima verba*.

How is it that we have these records? Certainly not because there was an urge to produce for publication a biography of Jesus. Whatever these records are – we call them 'gospels' because they are unique literary pieces – they are certainly not biographies. 'Portraits' might be a suitable description. So we have four portraits of Jesus; and this is significant: for all the differences in style and content, yes, even with some contradictions of detail, they are all recognizable of the same Jesus. There need be no doubt, we can know from the four gospels what Jesus was like.

The question still remains, however, why were they written? The date of the earliest is at least thirty years after the events it records. And how was it that the Church kept going for so long without these records? Why was there an urge at last to produce them? One urge must surely have been the necessity to meet the *pastoral* needs of the growing Christian congregations. They would need to know the Jesus who was proclaimed as Saviour. They would need to know him in whom they had believed, and in whose name they prayed, and of whose love they were assured. Perhaps there was real danger from fanciful stories about Jesus distorting the reality of his person and consequently enfeebling their faith. Let me make the point firmly. There cannot be authentic Christian faith in ignorance of the authentic portrait of Jesus, and there cannot be a distinctive life-style if he is virtually unknown. The knowledge of what Jesus was like had to be available, and certainly if there was to be any sense in such a statement as my text today makes – 'Jesus Christ, the same yesterday, today and for ever.'

3. Discipleship

And what does all this say to us? It says Christians must continue to be learners. A disciple is a learner. He is one who recognizes a Master and is willing to sit at his feet. Vague religious feeling is not enough. Knowledge there must also be, not to win eternal life for that is a gift received through faith, but in order to be able to apply it to daily living.

We need to know what Jesus said about prayer, about forgiveness, about riches, about covetousness, about adultery. We need imaginatively to see him touching the leper no one dared to touch; to see him putting his fingers in a deaf man's ear with the command 'be opened'; and wearing himself out with healing sessions for the crowds swarming around him; and sitting quietly talking to Mary of Bethany in her sister's house; and rebuking Simon the proud Pharisee so subtly; and talking straight yet with feeling to a woman divorced five times as he sat by a well in Samaria.

When we kneel down to pray, believing that we are in the presence of the risen Christ, this is the Christ we are encountering. 'He is the same yesterday, today and for ever.' And from these stories, from these pictures, we can know what God is like because Jesus was, is and always will be, the revelation of the Father.

Of all the stories in the gospels to which I might with profit draw your attention I will limit myself to three. They show us what the risen Christ is like and they all have to do with *listening*.

When at a wedding feast in Galilee – and such feasts in that culture might last for days – Mary the mother of Jesus went to tell him of the embarrassment caused by the wine running out, a strictly domestic predicament. Jesus *listened*, and in his own time and in his own way remedied the situation. When Simon Peter's wife's mother fell ill with a fever the family went and told Jesus. He *listened* to what they said and went at once to heal her. When Jairus the ruler of the synagogue sent a servant to tell Jesus that his daughter was seriously ill, he *listened* and followed the man at once to the house. Need I press the point? The risen Christ, the One in whose name we pray, listens when we take our concerns to him, be they never so humble, never so mundane, even improper or out of place. There is no one more competent to recognize and reject the unworthy prayer than the Lord himself, but we are encouraged to bring before God whatever our needs may be. I know petitionary prayer is not the whole of prayer. I know too how intercessions can become self-centred. But God listens when we pray. And God acts as he wills in response to our prayers. We shall only know this or ever dare to believe this if we become disciples however, that is, learners of Christ by reading, hearing and thinking over the stories we have in the gospels. And if preachers could make these stories live in their preaching, what an impetus this would provide for the interior spiritual life and the exterior life-style in the world.

'Jesus Christ is the same yesterday, today and for ever.' Yes, the risen Christ is dependable, he is knowable and we can 'learn of him'. What confidence is generated by this shining text. Say it out loud when the sea of life gets rough. Keep enough final breath at the close of life's span to say it once more, for it will give us peace at the last. 'Jesus Christ is the same yesterday, today, and for ever.'

15. The God who Seeks

Revelation 3.20 (RSV) *Behold, I stand at the door and knock.*

What an odd text. God standing outside the door of our life and seeking to come in! Does God do this? Isn't the truth rather that we have to seek him, we have to knock on the door of his presence? Isn't this what Isaiah 55.6 teaches, 'Seek ye the Lord while he may be found, call ye upon him while he is near'? And the Sermon on the Mount, 'Ask, and ye shall receive; seek and ye shall find; knock and it shall be opened.' We are the ones who have to do the seeking and the knocking.

1. The God who seeks

And if our text presents a contrary picture it must be admitted that people, since the world began, have been slow to accept it, and still are. God doesn't seek us, he can't; he is a fixed, immovable, inscrutable Being, if indeed he is a being at all and not a thing or a mental concept. So on the one hand idols have been fashioned to represent God, and they can't move and knock on people's doors, they have to *be* moved. And on the other hand God has been represented as a philosophical abstraction such as The First Cause, or The Ground of our Being, or The Sum Total of our loftiest human ideals. Thus if God is not a thing, he is at least an 'It', all of which makes our text 'Behold I stand at the door and knock' first class nonsense.

But is it nonsense? What if Easter is true and God is after all the living God! And what if Good Friday is true and God is not only the living God but the caring God, the loving God! What kind of a picture is proper then? One who stands at the door and knocks? And how should we answer the knocking?

Let me offer you such a picture, a bit rough maybe since it is in story form, but not worthless. It comes from Hugh Miller's recent book *The Giving Heart* and tells of a Welsh girl called

Megan broken-hearted by the telegram regretfully announcing the death of her fiancé in the trenches in World War I. There was, however, an unplanned child of their desperate passionate farewell before he left for the Front, a not uncommon occurrence in those bleak years 1914–18; and the care of the growing child gradually lifted the gloom from Megan's life. But another blow fell. After some eighteen months the child was taken suddenly ill and died. This second loss all but finished Megan; wearily she dragged through her days growing uncharacteristically morose. Then months later a man knocked on her door (so to speak). They knew each other well, indeed the man loved her deeply and longed to marry her, and this she knew. He had delayed calling for fear a visit, if only to sympathize, might be premature, which it was. She spoke to him, but that is all she did. She said had he telephoned before making his long journey to call he might have saved his rail fare. So the door was shut; his knocking had been of no use; his love was not wanted. Megan preferred her grief.

Now my question – can we, dare we compare God to the man seeking Megan in her trouble? and can we, dare we see ourselves in the kind of response Megan gave? Certainly the great Saint Augustine could because he asks in the first chapter of his *Confessions*, that great spiritual classic of all time, 'What am I to thee, that thou shouldest demand my love?'

So Easter rightly stands all those notions of God being a fixed immovable thing we have to seek, on their heads! Read the Easter stories in the gospels. Did anyone need to go seeking and searching the risen Christ till they found him? Yes, indeed, Mary Magdalene and the other woman went looking in his grave, but he wasn't there, so the scriptures say. On the contrary, the risen Christ accosted Mary in the garden. He also sought out poor miserable, self-recriminating Peter, and to the two travellers on the road to Emmaus he finally disclosed himself. Then there were the eleven disciples behind locked doors, terrified of possible apprehension on account of their association with the crucified Jesus, but all at once he appeared in their midst. And as if this isn't enough to dispel the idea that

God is an 'It' immovable and fixed, we read of the risen Christ turning up on the beach by the Galilean lake and calling out to seven disciples in a fishing boat, 'Friends have you any fish?'

Of course you may explain these incidents as you will, but one thing you must admit, God is being presented here not as a thing or an 'It' whom we have to seek but as One who seeks us, or in the words of our text, 'Behold, I stand at the door and knock'.

2. The God who meets our need

But why does God seek us out and knock on the door of our life? What does he want? What is he after? Is it to reprove us, to correct and punish us? Let us look again at these Easter stories.

The first story we have is of the risen Christ making himself known to Mary *because* she was broken by bereavement. He spoke her name as no one else spoke it – Mary! Then he appeared to Peter skulking in hiding *because* he had let his Master down: next to two disciples disillusioned *because* the crucifixion of Jesus had dashed their hopes of national liberation. And the disciples in the upper room were closeted there afraid. And the seven disciples in the fishing boat on the lake of Galilee were seven men who felt their lives to be empty of purpose.

What message are these stories crying aloud to tell us? Surely that God comes and stands outside the door of our lives most frequently when we are down, almost at breaking point. It is at those times that all of us are most open to this possibility. Ask any hospital chaplain; even the non-religious tend to ask religious questions then.

And if as seems indisputable, for all the pleasure-seeking of the present age, there exists in the community at large an underlying malaise and unhappiness (which manifests itself in various forms, many of them strident), then God must be standing outside the door of our people now, knocking, knocking, knocking.

78

An example of inner unhappiness camouflaged by strident behaviour was told me not long ago. It concerned a boy in a large comprehensive school who upset the whole classroom daily till even the other pupils, let alone the teacher, wearied of him. Then he asked if he could bring his dog to school. It seemed a monstrous request and against all the rules. But in desperation as to what to do with this boy the head finally agreed. So there sat the dog by the boy's desk, and the boy was no more trouble. Why? Simply because the dog gave him significance since it would sit by no one else; and significance is what he had lacked all his life in the wretched, quarrelsome home from which he came. And God of course sees below the noisy secularism of our times. He knows too the bitter taste of rejection, for was not Christ rejected by his generation and crucified? He also stands by the door of our life when we are gloriously happy and the sun is shining bright; but when the clouds thicken and the storms break he knocks and knocks again so that he may enter bringing his consolation and his strength to meet our need whatever it is. 'Behold, I stand at the door and knock.' And how do we answer? Like Megan in my story? You need not have bothered to come! or with the simple prayer which is all that is required, 'Even so, come Lord Jesus'.

3. The last knock

And now the moment when God will knock for the last time. It will be to call us home. There is a solemnity about this knock and I do not wish to dwell on it, but this I must say; that summons will be to a life more glorious than this, and without its sorrows, its tears and its pains. The resurrection of Christ proclaims it.

A few days ago the wonder of this struck me in an unexpected way. The time and the occasion was choral evensong broadcast from Manchester Cathedral. It was the Canticles that really affected me. They were sung to Wood in F

(*Collegium regale*). And the Nunc Dimittis, 'Lord now lettest thou thy servant depart in peace' came over as the old man accepting his final call, so gentle, so sobering. And then, all of a sudden, a great burst of song for the Gloria. Up and up it went, soaring, pealing, almost bursting; and the Amen seemed as if it couldn't stop itself – Amen, Amen, Amen. What was this? The composer showing off what he could do? It was then that I understood what he was saying. When we come to the end of our lives and the Lord knocks for the last time, it will be to pass through the door of death into unspeakable resurrection glory. What a message there was in the music! What an Easter message! What a proclamation of the risen Christ! 'When Christ, who in our life, shall appear, then shall ye also appear with him in glory', wrote St Paul to the Christians in Colossae (Colossians 3.4). 'Behold, I stand at the door and knock: if anyone hears my voice, and opens the door, I will come in to him, and eat with him, and he with me. He who conquers, I will grant him to sit with me on my throne as I myself conquered and sat down with my Father on his throne. He who has an ear let him hear what the Spirit says to the Churches' (Revelation 3.20–22).

16. The Risen and Exalted Christ

Philippians 2.9 (NEB) *Therefore God raised him to the heights.*

Some months ago there appeared in one of the national newspapers an article which attempted to discover how Jews recognize their affinity with each other even if they are as far apart politically, socially and culturally as Karl Marx and Disraeli. Is it race, religion, or sense of destiny? The writer dismissed all three as sufficient explanation and suggested instead a peculiar quality of intelligence. The Jews, he asserted, have a remarkable capacity for reasoning, especially in its abstract and philosophical form. This shows up especially in advanced mathematics and science, and their technological application, and this distinctive intelligence Jews recognize in each other. Whatever the truth of this, and it will be fiercely debated, it is remarkable how many Jews have captured top posts in the academic world of the West; especially remarkable when the fact is borne in mind that until little more than a century ago they were barred from access to the universities, being locked in the narrow culture of the ghetto. Story after story can be told of the rise of individuals to eminence from homes where no books were available other than the Hebrew scriptures, and they achieved this regardless of the difference in language and culture.

For myself I can't help wondering if the influence of these very Hebrew scriptures are not part of the explanation. Jewish children have been reared for centuries on the stories they contain. What is more, unless we have looked into the matter we have no idea of the respect, almost amounting to awe, with which the scholar was held in the ghetto life of Jewry. Children would be taken along to the room (and there was little spare space in a ghetto), where the scholars were studying in order that they might peep in and observe this wonderful sight of grown men poring over their books. And if the intellectual soil of the Jew was naturally fertile who can tell what influence the story of Joseph, for example, would have on him as it was read over and over again till he knew it by heart?

Do you remember the story? It can be retold in outline in a few words. Joseph was an intelligent lad who got sold into slavery in Egypt by his brothers jealous of his precocity. Yet even as a slave he quickly rose to a position of trust in his master's household. There, however, he was falsely accused by his master's wife of trying to seduce her, as a result of which he found himself in prison. But here too, as a prisoner, he rose to a position of responsibility. For two years he languished in gaol till at last his intelligence and his charisma of being able to interpret dreams brought him to the attention of Pharaoh and he found himself appointed as governor over all the land of Egypt, living in the style of royalty. This story of the rise of a boy from a humble background to the heights, his foreign language and culture notwithstanding, was dinned into the children of every Jewish household. How many are there that have made this story their own?

1. The Resurrection

I want to suggest that this Old Testament story of Joseph is a picture of Jesus in so far as it illustrates the great theme of exaltation. Of Joseph it could properly be said that 'God raised him to the heights', and that is exactly what is said of Jesus in Philippians chapter 2.9. Let us hear the whole passage where this phrase occurs:

> For the divine nature was his from the first; yet he did not think to snatch at equality with God, but made himself nothing, assuming the nature of a slave. Bearing the human likeness, revealed in human shape, he humbled himself, and in obedience accepted even death – death on a cross. Therefore God raised him to the heights and bestowed on him the name above all names, that at the name of Jesus every knee should bow – in heaven, on earth, and in the depths – and every tongue confess, 'Jesus Christ is Lord', to the glory of God the Father.

I began by reminding you of how many Jews by the exercise of their intelligence in spite of initial disadvantages, have raised themselves to exalted positions in the modern world. The story of Joseph in the Old Testament is similar as regards the exaltation from lowly origins but it is dissimilar in one most important respect – all the emphasis is thrown on to the belief that God was the instigator and controller of elevation. It was God's doing that brought Joseph into his exalted position in Egypt.

And so it is in the story of Jesus. He did not raise himself up; he did not snatch at equality with God. On the contrary, he humbled himself. He went down, down to human likeness and human shape, and further still down to death and that of the most ignominious kind, death on the cross, and all this trusting in the rightness of it as God's will for him; whereafter God raised him up. He raised him up from death. The resurrection of Jesus is the first part of this exaltation, and the exaltation is the consequence of God's acceptance of his obedience. Listen to the text again, '*Therefore* God raised him to the heights'. Thus the risen Christ is the exalted Lord. He is that *as risen*.

2. The Ascension

I think it may be wise for us to pause here for a moment. It has been my experience – and doubtless of many others as well – to see quite a few people 'get on in the world', as we say. The result is top positions, more money, an elevated life-style. Some of them, I am sorry to say, put on airs, cutting themselves off from their old associates. These people have become exalted in the wrong sense, and the figure they cut is not attractive. It seems to me that the stories about Jesus after his resurrection go out of their way to show that he was not exalted in this fashion at all. On the contrary, on a number of occasions he appeared to his old associates, indeed he did not appear to anyone else. It was Mary Magdalene that he met, and Simon Peter and all eleven apostles. And in what ordinary situations! – in a garden looking like a gardener, as a solitary walker on a country road, as a man by the lakeside preparing a meal on an open fire. What are these stories saying? They are proclaiming the truth about the exalted Christ that he is not exalted above fellowship with ordinary sinful men and women. The risen Christ – this is the important lesson for us – is with us in a spiritual sense as he was with his disciples in Galilee and Judaea in a physical sense. As far as Christ is concerned, his appearances after his resurrection were quite unnecessary. They took place for two reasons at least; one, to show that he is alive, and two, to show that his exaltation to life beyond death does not separate him from the dwellers on earth.

It took time for these lessons to sink in to the consciousness of the apostles – St Luke says forty days (a favourite Biblical phrase for the time) – and then what has come to be called the. ascension closed the succession of resurrection appearances. The ascension was part of Christ's exaltation. As risen he was already exalted but the teaching period took place to establish the truth that the risen and exalted Christ, though henceforth invisible to physical sight, was not exalted away from his people; he is with them, he is with us still.

3. The elevation to the throne of God

And now we can see the third part of Christ's exaltation. The risen and ascended Christ is raised to the very throne of God himself. Listen to the scripture passage again from Philippians chapter 2: 'Therefore God raised him to the heights and bestowed on him the name above all names, that at the name of Jesus every knee should bow – in heaven, on earth, and in the depths – and every tongue confess, "Jesus Christ is Lord", to the glory of God the Father.'

What a long way we have come from the baby in the manger at Bethlehem, the man of Galilee sometimes 'with nowhere to lay his head', and the tormented victim on the cross at Golgotha! The titles Son of Man, the man for others, brother man, even teacher and reconciler, will not suffice any longer. Christ is the King, the one with the name above all other names, he to whom it is fitting to bow the knee in worship. Christ is on the throne of God.

And so it comes about that Easter is the time for worship, Christian worship, worship of the risen and exalted Christ. And so Sunday came to replace the Jewish Sabbath (Saturday) as the weekly Easter and the weekly day for worship. We show that we believe in the resurrection of Christ by worshipping on Sundays, not least by the hymns we sing –

> Christ is the King! O friends rejoice;
> Brothers and sisters, with one voice
> Make all men know he is your choice,
> > Alleluia.
> > (G.K.A. Bell 1883–1958)

This captures the authentic note of Christianity – joy and rejoicing, such joy and rejoicing that the urge to tell everyone the world over the good news of the risen and exalted Christ. Buoyant and outgoing this is the hallmark of Christian people who have taken hold of the exaltation of Jesus in their hearts and minds. 'God raised him to the heights.' Alleluia. No wonder we preach the Risen Christ.

17. The Church in the Risen Christ

Colossians 1.18 (NEB) *He is, moreover, the head of the body, the Church. He is its origin, the first to return from the dead, to be in all things alone supreme.*

One of the strange experiences of growing older is the way in which odd and insignificant incidents from the past stick vividly in the memory. I recall, as if it were yesterday, how when I was a student a fellow student (also from Norfolk as I was), visited my room in college with the unexpected request that I should help him to understand the apostle Paul; 'I go to these lectures on the Epistle to the Romans' he complained, 'but I just can't make out what Paul was driving at'. Why he should have come to me, I do not know, but he did. After all he wasn't unintelligent. He was a well set up six-footer who, after ordination, did good work as a chaplain in a Guards Regiment during the war and ended up as an archdeacon before he died. But he wasn't the first to find Paul difficult, nor the last. I find him difficult, so apparently did the author of the Second Epistle of Peter in the New Testament itself (see 3.16). And maybe one of Paul's most difficult ideas for modern ears is his teaching on the Church as the body of the Risen Christ. To this however we must give our attention.

1. The Church as a building

I guess I should not be far wrong if I suggested that the Church is most commonly thought of as a building at the corner of some street or facing the village green where cricket is 'wont to be played'. In all probability it is one of the few pieces of distinctive architecture in the neighbourhood; and if it is a cathedral, it is far away the biggest tourist attraction. It is of course expensive to maintain, sometimes cripplingly expensive. Even so, church buildings are not dispensable. They perform a spiritual function simply by standing there. People

identify with them, even people who rarely, if ever, attend a
service of worship. This is why they will help to contribute
financially to their maintenance. The Kent miners, not
renowned for their religious fervour, contributed generously to
the fund for restoring Canterbury Cathedral. The church
building operates as a visible sign to the community that there
is a spiritual dimension to our human existence. A community
without a church building is a community bereft of life-lines
when tragedy strikes, and the going gets rough, not least when
we come to the end of our day. Some people, many people,
only guess at this from the outside, but it may impel them to
give to the fabric fund or help cut the churchyard grass in the
summer. This identification, even this bare identification,
saves them. Yes, indeed, to conceive of the church merely in
terms of bricks and mortar is elementary, but we must not
destroy the building at the end of the street or facing the village
green. It functions as a spiritual agent in ways beyond those
which the unreflective could ever imagine.

2. The Church as a company of people

A deeper understanding of the Church is the recognition of it
as the company of all God's faithful people, that is, the people
of faith in the God and Father of our Lord Jesus Christ. In
other words, the Church consists not of bricks and mortar but
of people. It is a living temple, a living building, a visible
assembly of living people, a community of faith in the Risen
Christ. We come to belong to it through baptism and are
nourished in it by the ministry of the word of God and the
sacrament of holy communion, all of which implies the
existence of clergy to serve it. Sometimes people think of the
clergy as 'the Church'. They say of a prospective ordinand – 'he
is going into the Church'. The Church, however, is not the
clergy, it is the whole body of Christian believers, men and
women of flesh and blood, liable to temptation and liable to
fall.

Note this liability. The Church though an assembly of men and women of faith in the Risen Christ is not therefore an assembly of saints in the sense of being perfect. It is an assembly of people called *to be saints*. And they find it tough going. I ought to say, we find it tough going. It is so because we are sinners, still struggling and often failing to live up to the pattern set by the Lord Christ. There is no such organization anywhere in the world as a perfect Church.

I have told this story before, but I will tell it again. A young man came for an interview with Charles Haddon Spurgeon, the great Victorian preacher who at the Metropolitan Tabernacle in South London used to hold a regular congregation of six thousand, sometimes ten thousand. The young man said he was looking for the perfect Church. Was the Metropolitan Tabernacle such a place? 'No' replied Spurgeon. 'There are some very saintly people in this Church, devoted and self-sacrificing Christians; but there are also some time-servers, some hypocrites, and some scarcely worthy of the name "Christian".' (At least this is the tenor of his reply). 'No' he went on, 'this is not a perfect Church, but if ever, young man, you should find such a place, though I doubt it, I beg of you *not* to join it, because the moment you do it will become an imperfect Church like all the others.'

The Church is a great world-wide community composed of people of all races, languages and cultures, sinners every one; but they are sinners forgiven in the name of the crucified and risen Christ who is worshipped as Lord and Master in churches of all shapes, sizes and architectural styles.

3. The Church in Christ

And now we are come to the distinctive teaching of St Paul as contained in my text, 'He (Christ) is, moreover, the head of the body, the Church. He is its origin, the first to return from the dead, to be in all things alone supreme.' Here we have the idea of the Church as the body of Christ. It owes its origin to the resurrection of Christ. It is the Church of the Risen Christ. More than that, the Church is the assembly in which Christ is risen. He is risen there in the preached word and in the administration of the sacraments; he is also there in the fellowship of believers. We are not, however, to *equate* the risen Christ with the Church as if they were identical, which would result in ecclesiastical triumphalism. No, the risen Christ, as well as being in the Church, is beyond the Church, as its head.

Is this too hard to understand? Is it too theological for an ordinary congregation? This we can all grasp: the Church is to be reckoned on a higher plane than merely bricks and mortar, a higher plane even than a unity of living people with a common faith in Christ as Lord, (although it is both of these); the Church is to be recognized as the body of the Risen Christ (of which he is the head) and wherein his risen life is known.

Even this is not all. There is a phrase in St Paul's writing which occurs over and over again; 'in Christ'. An example is 2 Corinthians 5.17 (RSV): 'Wherefore if any man is in Christ, he is a new creature'. So we are not only to understand the risen Christ as *in the Church* but also that the Church is *in the risen Christ*. This implies that Christ is not only an individual but a corporate personality. Christians are *in Christ* and this incorporation is what makes the Church a *corpus*, that is, a body, alive with the aliveness of Christ.

I know this is hard to grasp and it is hard for me as the preacher to find an illustration which will make it any easier. Here, however, is a house up for sale. You are intrigued to see who the new occupants will be, not least because the outgoing owners let it go to rack and ruin. The paintwork is peeling, the garden overgrown, the windows so dirty it is to be wondered if the daylight could ever penetrate them. And then the new owners arrive. In a matter of weeks the place is almost unrecognizable. What is more, a year later it is still being maintained in its fresh condition of cleanliness and smartness. Why the change? The reason is obvious. New people are *in the house*. Yes but the house is also now *in the new people*. It has been taken up into their way of life, into their concern for order and cleanliness, into their discipline and energy. An inadequate illustration, maybe, but it may help us to see how the Church is in Christ when Christ is in it.

Need we ordinary church people bother our heads over abstract considerations such as these? Certainly not if we are content with a small version of our faith, seeing the Church as only a building of bricks and mortar, or a fellowship of like-minded people. But a small version of our faith makes for small Christians and small Christians make only a very small impact on a non-Christian world. The call is to deepen our Christian understanding of the Church to which we belong so that we may wield a bigger influence in our contemporary society which has lost its way. This is why we need to see the Church for what it is, the body of the risen Christ of which he is the Lord.

18. Two Men – Two Consequences

1 Corinthians 15.21 (RSV)   *As by a man came death, by a man has come also the resurrection of the dead.*

In a book entitled *Julie* by Catherine Marshall there is a story about the proprietor of a local newspaper called *The Sentinel* printed and circulated in Alderton, a small steel works town in the United States of America. The struggle to get the paper going was intense, and the proprietor and his family were often in desperate financial straits. To make matters worse the powerful owner of the steel works became hostile to the paper because it dared to criticize some of the working conditions in his mills. He determined to crush it, stooping to such mean tricks as attempting to burn down the printing plant and poisoning the proprietor's daughter's dog which was the light of her life. The little girl was heartbroken, and there was no soothing her sorrow except to carry the dead dog out into the garden for burial with the full funeral service as if the deceased were a person. It was a most touching scene, and one you and I would have been willing to organize although knowing quite well that there is a great difference between the death of a human being and the death of an animal.

Somehow the death of an animal is natural. Yes, of course we miss the old horse sorely, and the dog, and even the cat. The place doesn't seem the same without Dobbin and Rusty and Tibby: they have become part of our lives. But the death of a human being is different. There is a terror in it: it seems all wrong. After all we are not like animals. Animals cannot talk, reason or even laugh. Why then do we have to die like them? We would expect something different to happen in our case; but it doesn't – or does it? Perhaps we should be wise to turn to the New Testament in order to try and find out. And so to my text, 'As by a man came death, by a man has come also the resurrection of the dead'.

1. The first man

Here we are introduced to two different men from whom flow two different consequences. Neither is given a name in this text and when we do supply them they operate differently. The first man is Adam and the second man is Jesus of Nazareth. This is clear from the verse which follows 'For as in Adam all die, so also in Christ shall all be made alive'. But Adam is not the name of a particular person who lived a long time ago, whereas the name 'Jesus' does refer to an historical person, as historical as the Roman Emperor Tiberius in whose reign he lived. Adam is the Hebrew word for Man. 'Since by man came death' is how the Authorized Version translates this text, not 'a man'. The reference is to the human race. We are all *in* Adam. Adam is in all of us. We are Adam. And the same prospect lies before us all. In due time death will be our common experience – 'As in Adam all die', so reads the verse next to my text in 1 Corinthians chapter 15.21.

Why do we have to die? Because we cannot arrest the progressive wearing out of our physical bodies, or arrange that no virus shall attack us any more, nor street accident befall us. We are subject to our physical bodies. This is how it is to be 'in Adam'. Or if we wish to express the truth in picture language, we could say we are part of one vast crowd of human beings called Adam, the universal man, and what happens to him happens to us all.

There is, moreover, another complicating factor. We are unlike animals in that we have a moral dimension to our lives. We know what sin is, and by this I do not simply mean that we all tend to perform wrong actions at times and think wrong thoughts. I mean we are born into a social order which is already self-centred and not God-centred. In this sense we are 'in Adam' and so our moral judgement is distorted from the start. And we acquiesce in it, and even seek to justify it. It is this moral dimension, this sin-awareness that makes for the distinctive bitterness of human death. We know we are not all we might be and yet to some extent we can't help being what we are. So we are trapped. And the death of the trapped is what accounts for much of the poignancy. Every human deathbed speaks of human powerlessness. We know we have to die, and our loved ones have to die, and all to a greater or lesser degree as sinners. Our tears express more than our bereavement. They struggle with our embarrassment: we are confused and definitely ill at ease.

2. The second man

This is where I have to stop; we all have to stop. There is nothing more to add to our human story except perhaps a postscript telling of how since the world began people have refused to believe that death really is the end, inventing myths and philosophies proclaiming human immortality. And then we pick up the New Testament, turn to 1 Corinthians chapter 15.21 and read this: 'As by a man came death, by a man has come also the resurrection of the dead.'

Everything here turns on 'the man' that is Jesus Christ. It is he who makes the difference. What we have here is not an argument for human immortality in spite of all appearances; we are by nature mortal; only God is *by nature* immortal. What could be clearer than 1 Timothy 6.16? 'He (God) is King of kings and Lord of lords; he alone possesses immortality, dwelling in unapproachable light.'

There is an idea abroad, and has been for a very long time, that a human being is composed of two *separate* parts. He is indeed composed of two parts – body and soul – but they are not, according to the Bible, and I would say according to reason, *separable*. Nor are we to say that one part, the body, is mortal, and the other part, the soul, is immortal. The soul is not therefore a kind of spirit, or ghost, housed within a physical container called the body which at death breaks up thus setting free the soul to fly out and inhabit a world of disembodied spirits. This (or something like this) was ancient Greek thought, but it is not New Testament thought. Were it so there would be no need of Christ, for part of man would be *by nature* immortal anyway. No, a human being is psycho-somatic creature, a body-soul complex destined for death. Whether or not the human personality (that is the soul) may survive the death of the body at least for a time I do not know beyond what reputable psychical researchers assert. In any case what we are considering here is immortality and how it does not belong to man *by nature*.

But then into this grey area of uncertainty there appears the second man changing the entire situation and prospect: 'As by a man came death, by a man has come also the resurrection of the dead'. This second man was a real man, that is to say he was a complex psychosomatic whole as we all are, body and soul knit together into one, each part affecting the whole. And he too was liable to death, and in fact did die, was buried, and placed in a garden tomb. But God raised him from the dead; body and soul was raised to a newness of life, not (be it noted) to the old life revivified but to a resurrection life. So resurrec-tion 'has come', to use the wording of our text. It has come with Jesus Christ. Everything turns on this second man.

3. The gospel of resurrection

So now we have a gospel, good news to tell. Resurrection to eternal life if what the future holds beyond the grave. And because everything turns on the risen Christ, the gospel calls for a response. It bids us put ourselves on his side. We may call this the response of faith, and what it does is to bind us to him, so when we come to die we die *bound to him*, the Christ who died; but because he rose from death we too shall rise.

Have I expressed faith too loosely in speaking of 'being on the side of Christ'? I have done so on purpose. Of course I am aware that only an intelligent and active union of heart and mind to the risen Christ produces the transformed life now, but the gospel is also properly expounded in its breadth when it declares that the slightest step in the direction of Christ brings with it the gift of God's grace – resurrection to eternal life beyond the grave.

Not long ago I was working with a man helping to pile garden refuse on a bonfire. He was not a bad man but could not in any sense be called a religious man. His consuming interests were horse-racing, darts and gambling machines. But with evident satisfaction he told me of a recent 'find', as he called it, at a car boot sale, 'a lovely brass cross' he said, 'and on it a figure of Jesus'. I was taken aback, more surprised than if he had used the divine name blasphemously. Clearly he warmed to this 'find' and unwittingly let it be seen on whose side he was in his heart of hearts, mostly kept tight shut. There are millions of people like that man who was helping me with the bonfire: they will rise to eternal life and all because of the 'second man' we have been considering today, the risen Christ.

What is the measure of the love of God? One of the post-Easter New Testament readings is Luke 7.11–17. It intrigues me. Two crowds were approaching one another at the town gate of a place called Nain. The one was on its way to the cemetery outside, the other attempting to pass through inside. The one was headed by a widow weeping, the other by Jesus heading an enthusiastic following. They met head on. The key to the incident is what comes next: 'When the Lord saw her his heart went out to her, and he said "Weep no more".' He knew only too well how little was left in life for a widow then, and if it was her only son who was being carried out to his burial, almost nothing. So he brought the young man back to life. Why? The woman made no appeal. She gave no evidence of explicit or even implicit faith. We do not know if she had been a bad woman or a good woman. The whole action hinges on one fact and one only, 'When the Lord saw her his heart went out to her'. Tell me now, what is the measure of the love of God? It is this story which will not allow me to set any limits to God's gift of eternal life. It rests on God's compassion and this does not operate by calculation.

19.   Life through Death

1 Corinthians 15.36 (NEB)   *The seed you sow does not come to life unless it has first died.*

Yesterday I carried out a task which thousands of other people carry out at this time of year. It was 28 February. I spread a newspaper on my desk, brought in from the greenhouse twenty small plastic pots filled with damp seed-sowing compost, and then with a pair of tweezers sowed eleven geranium seeds and nine tomato seeds in them. After this, having covered them with transparent polythene, I carried the little tray load and (with the permission of my wife!) placed them in the bathroom airing cupboard where, in the warmth and dark they will, I trust (note the word) germinate. So in due course I expect to have fruit and flowers – the object of the exercise.

Nothing very remarkable in that, you say, so why tell us? I do so in order to make the point that the resurrection about which we think at Easter is not only a historical even nor future hope, nor even now a spiritual experience; it is a pattern of life in general. Life does not proceed without the death/resurrection cycle, of which spring is the annual reminder: or to put the matter another way; there cannot be life unless there is first of all death. So my text from 1 Corinthians 15.36 'The seed you sow does not come to life unless it has first died'.

1. Personal relationships

Take first the realm of personal relationships. Most of us rub shoulders (as we say) with scores and scores of people. They are of all shapes, sizes, temperaments and characters. We meet them through our work, our leisure, our shopping, our recreations, our business and our parties. In all probability we know next to nothing about those whom we encounter in these ways. I once was in contact with a professional man who was legal adviser to one of the biggest of our nationalized industries. One

95

day he was telling me about his chief clerk when, for what reason I cannot remember, I asked 'Is he married?' – 'Good gracious' he replied, looking half amused, half embarrassed, 'Do you know, I have no idea, I have never thought about it.' Yet they had met across a desk daily for years! I can't imagine a parallel situation with a woman! And he was a very likeable and estimable man.

Most of us have scores and scores of acquaintances. Some people in what are called 'high positions' have hundreds: but how many friends? I gather that many, if not most of the latter have very few indeed, if any. In these cases it may be the result of deliberate policy. After all if you have friends you have to open your heart, at least a little, and the moment you do this you are vulnerable. You may be betrayed. You may be let down. And then you suffer for it, not only inside in your feelings but outside in your circumstances. So there are leaders who purposely have no friends, but only acquaintances. The price for this is high; one is loneliness, although some men, and maybe some women (I don't know) think prudence demands that they pay it.

When then do acquaintances turn into friends? When, out of the many with whom we rub shoulders, do a few qualify to bear this title? I mean in the strict sense. Maybe I ought to use the phrase 'real friends'. In order to answer this question, let us take a concrete situation. Here is a man who has run into trouble, serious trouble. It is not his fault. There is nothing he could have done to avoid what has happened. And one day you meet him unexpectedly. He looks thinner and rather older than when last you met. You get talking about his misfortune, indeed the subject can hardly be avoided because you know him so well. After a while, shrugging his shoulders and looking vacantly into the distance he says, half to himself, 'I'll tell you what, when things go wrong you can tell who your friends are.' And then after a pause, 'and who they are not.'

Isn't this the truth? Friends, or perhaps I ought to adhere to the phrase 'real friends' are they who stand by you when the going gets rough, whether that roughness be occasioned by illness, disappointment, bereavement or financial ruin. It is not the jolly fellows who stand by you then, unless there is something more in them than jollity. It is not the ones who profited by you or whom you have profited. It is not even those with whom you share some common interests. Real friends are they who have become so by keeping close to you when you were in trouble. This is so true that we can go on to say that it is the sharing of trouble that makes for real friendship. This does not mean there are no stretches of fun, laughter and intellectual stimulus, but unless there is some mutual opening of the heart in adversity, be it mental or circumstantial, no real friendship is born, only a variation of acquaintanceship. All of which proclaims the message that without sorrow shared there is no deep joy, without death there is no resurrection. 'The seed you sow does not come to life unless it has first died.' The crucifixion was the means by which God in Christ came close to us in our sorrow and sinfulness. The resurrection with its joy was only possible because of the death. This, I repeat, is not only true of that historical event, it is a pattern of life. It can be seen in operation for example in the realm of personal relationships.

2. Resurrection requires faith

And now I invite you to think a stage further. Adversity may be the means of rising to a higher quality of life for which the description 'resurrection' is not inappropriate but – and this is a very real 'but' – the change is neither automatic nor inevitable; there has to be faith to make it happen.

Take first of all an elementary example of such faith. It comes from a novel by Philip Gibbs, the title of which escapes me. In it is the story of a young and promising violinist in Moscow when the Communist pressures upon normal life were at some of their harshest. He did not know how he could continue with his studies, everything seemed against him; he was cold, hungry and lonely. And meeting an older man, old enough to be his father, he sought comfort from him as he recounted his sorry tale of woe. But what comfort could the man give? There was no likelihood of amelioration in the living conditions in Soviet Russia then. Yet he did have a message for him, a strong message. Placing his hands on the young man's shoulders, and looking him straight in the eyes he said, 'All this will be good for your violin'. What was he doing? He was seeking to evoke the young man's faith in himself, in his talent, in the worthwhileness of his musical career. Without that faith, be it only elementary, he would be crushed by his hardships, but with it resurrection to new life out of the very same hardships would be possible. And in this context it meant a richer expression of art; fuller, deeper, touching more the hidden recesses of the human spirit. Perhaps there is no art, whether musical, pictorial or literary which has not in some measure arisen out of travail: 'Except a corn of wheat fall into the ground and die, it abideth by itself alone: but if it die, it beareth much fruit' – the words of our Lord in John 12.24. In our experience this takes place through faith. Does not even the non-religious gardener have faith about the seeds he sows, and the directions on the seed merchants' seed packet?

And so the Church seeks to encourage great faith, faith beyond ourselves, faith in God, faith in the power of God, the guidance of God, the compassion of God, and his concern for ordinary mortals such as we are, a concern stretching down to the details of our lives. And why does the Church proclaim such faith? Is it because faith is (so to speak) its stock in trade? No, it is so that the setbacks, frustrations and sorrows of our lives may have the possibility of being turned into places of resurrection and newness of life. This resurrection can be when we approach them in faith. It is part of the good news of the Easter tidings.

3. Self-denial

And now a third consideration. To rise to newness of life in the rough stretches of our lives we need not only faith but a readiness to die to self, to self-centredness, and selfishness. This is hard. We do not like dying to self. In a sense it is unnatural. From infancy we are by nature self-centred: our little world is dominated by what we want and what we have. Some people never grow out of this, indeed it is doubtful if self-centredness is a disposition out of which we do *naturally* grow. We need to be shown the way, and shown the reason for the way; and then to make the necessary effort.

Of course there are those for whom the very notion of self-denial is ridiculous. 'If you do not fight for yourself' they say, 'nobody else will . . . and doesn't the weakest go to the wall?' If this means that self-centredness is strength, it is a fallacy. The self-centred are prisoners and narrow in perspective. Or, as I once heard it expressed, 'Edith is like a very small parish bounded on all four sides by Edith'.

There is, however, a place where the principle of life through death *is* learned by nature; it is in motherhood. A mother's mind is not on herself, it is on her child. She comes *by nature* to sacrifice for it, and suffer for it, even to bend her whole life for the benefit of her little boy or girl. And through this self-denial she realizes in herself the joy of living; or as our Lord said, 'He that loseth his life shall find it'.

I come back to the seeds I sowed in my little plastic pots. I did not dampen the soil compost, I did not place the seeds in the dark as the final operation because I was aiming at disintegration, I was aiming at fruit and flowers to enjoy. And this is how we must understand God. He does not wish unhappiness, troubles or travail for us; the very reverse; but these are part of life as we experience it. And so there is proclaimed in nature this principle of life through death. 'The seed you sow does not come to life unlesss it has first died.' Above all it was enacted outside Jerusalem's walls in AD 29, or thereabouts, in the crucifixion and resurrection of Jesus. Life through death. We are called to witness this, to believe this and to apply it to the rough places of our daily lives. Through faith in God those rough places can be made plain, and the crooked made straight. Resurrection as well as a future hope can be a present experience now. Newness of life can be the outcome of brokenness through the power of the Risen Christ. This is the message of Easter.

20.   A Ridiculous Doctrine?

Matthew 22.31–33 (NEB)   *'But about the resurrection of the dead, have you never read what God himself said to you: "I am the God of Abraham, the God of Isaac, and the God of Jacob"? He is not God of the dead but of the living.' The people heard what he said, and were astounded at his teaching.*

I am not surprised that the crowds overhearing this altercation between Jesus and his opponents were astounded at his teaching. I guess we should have been astounded had we stood among them that day. It was a hot, blistering day. No, I do not mean as regards temperature, Fahrenheit or Celsius. I mean the atmosphere was boiling. It was like one of the worst question times in the House of Commons. Traps were being laid, smart traps designed to bring Jesus down. And in a way he started it. He implied in a neat story about guests rejecting an invitation to a wedding feast that this is what the nation had done with God's invitation to be his special people. It riled them. But they would get him; they must get him. So along they came with what they reckoned must be a winner; they would ask his views on paying taxes. No one likes paying taxes, least of all Jews paying taxes to Romans! Not on your life! But they didn't get Jesus. Very neatly he turned the question aside, leaving them standing – and smarting.

1. Ridicule

Another group was waiting to enter the ring, however, this time the Sadducees, a politicized sect. Their trap is what we shall consider now. It was about the resurrection. Seeing that the moralistic Pharisees had failed to get Jesus embroiled in political finance, they attempted doctrinal ridicule. They would make Jesus look silly. So along they came with a cock and bull story about a woman who had seven husbands, one

101

after another. A bawdy story about marriage is always good for a laugh with any crowd. So they spun out their story. One man married her and he died. Another married her and he died. So with all seven. Last of all the woman died also, and you can bet someone shouted, 'About time too!'; and another, 'What a woman!' But the Sadducees didn't trap Jesus. They didn't get him in the trap of ridicule any more than the Pharisees did in the trap of politics, in spite of their asking (oh so sweetly), 'In the resurrection whose wife shall she be of the seven, for they all had her as wife?'

How do you handle ridicule? Perhaps you have never been ridiculed for your faith. Perhaps unfortunately you haven't any faith about which you can be ridiculed. Perhaps you reckon that ridicule of the resurrection faith is non-existent in today's so-called civilized society. Then you must be living in a strange vacuum. Ask some factory worker what it is like being known as a churchman among his mates. Ask any boy or girl at a comprehensive school known to be a confirmation candidate. Ask a young student at a university trying to live by Christian moral standards. Is ridicule of the Christian faith dead today? No. But how is it to be handled?

2. Counter-attack

Come back to my story, today's second lesson from Matthew 22. Jesus did not allow those who ridiculed him to get away with the ridicule. He in fact charged them with ignorance – which is not the sort of charge rationalists, who pride themselves on their intelligence, like to hear. He said in effect, you conceive of resurrection as if it belongs to the present earthly existence where procreation is the order of the day through marriage of male and female, so of course you can make resurrection sound ridiculous. We can still do that. We can ask silly questions like where can there be sufficient space for all the resurrected who have existed down the ages to live? And isn't resurrection stupid anyway for at death our bodies get reincorporated in the stuff of the universe to appear in another · form? But resurrection is not resuscitation, and the whole concept anyway belongs to the transcendent world not to this.

Then Jesus drew his argument in; he pinned it on to the small section of the scripture his adversaries did confess to believe in. 'But about the resurrection of the dead, have you never read what God himself said to you: "I am the God of Abraham, the God of Isaac, and the God of Jacob"?' Of course they had read it. They had read it hundreds of times but they did not see fit to notice that God did not say, 'I *was* the God of Abraham, the God of Isaac, and the God of Jacob', but I *am* the God of these deceased people.

Let us pause here for a moment. Suppose, I say *suppose*, I stood in this pulpit* and said, 'I *was* a friend of the Archbishop of Canterbury', you would conclude that *either* I had ceased to be a friend and we had fallen out *or* that I was referring to an Archbishop now dead. But suppose instead of my saying 'I *was* a friend of the Archbishop', I said 'I *am* a friend of the Archbishop', it would never occur to you that I meant anyone else but the present *living* Archbishop; indeed we are both alive.

Now go back to my story. When Jesus reminded the Sadducees of what God had said in the Scripture 'I *am* the God of Abraham, the God of Isaac, and the God of Jacob' the implication has to be that though dead to this world, they are still alive.

Yes, I know that this may not be the kind of argument we would use today but the Sadducees understood it, and the crowd standing around understood it, and we too can understand it if we are willing. Jesus taught that the dead are not dead to God. They are not 'dead and done for', and for this reason that God is not God of the dead but of the living. And this is what almost all of us in our heart of hearts would like to believe, but too often we are argued out of this faith, or laughed out of it, or simply let it drift; and when the day comes that we need it it is simply not there.

* Canterbury Cathedral.

3. The Argument

(a) There are three points I should like to finish with on the basis of this story, and the first is that we shall not be in a position to counter those who ridicule our Christian faith if we are ignorant of what it really teaches. This is why a preaching/teaching ministry is necessary, perhaps urgently necessary today. We must know what we believe and be able to defend it. Or, as the first epistle of St Peter has it, 'being ready always to give an answer to every man that asketh you a reason of the hope that is in you'.

(b) Secondly, in the verbal battle with the Sadducees about the resurrection Jesus based his whole argument on the concept of friendship. Let me put it this way. Here is an experience familiar to most of us: a man falls in love with a girl. All right, let us make it really romantic and add 'at first sight'. Of course thereafter he will take trouble to get to know her. They meet, they talk, they discover more of each other's character. If then the love is real, what is the last thing they will allow to happen if they can possibly prevent it? Surely it is the break-up of the association, never to meet again. The truth is, love longs above all else to be with the loved one for ever. Now God has come close to us men and women in a relationship of love. He strengthens us, hears our prayer, guides us by his Spirit. This is what religion is all about or it is nothing. Can you imagine then that God wants that friendship to be broken? Can you imagine that he being God, the Sovereign Lord of life and death, will *allow* that friendship to be broken? 'I *am* the God' not 'I *was*'. And if you think those men were all oil paintings, read the book of Genesis. No wonder the psalmist sang in his day, 'Nevertheless, I am alway by thee: for thou hast holden me by my right hand. Thou shalt guide me with thy counsel: and after that receive me with glory' (Psalm 73.22, 23).

(c) This is a strong argument for the possibility – I said possibility – of life after death. Maybe it is the strongest argument that exists, and certainly the strongest the Old

Testament has to offer; indeed it is the strongest argument Jesus could employ with the Sadducees, for they thought in Old Testament categories. But this is by no means all now because Jesus himself has risen from the grave. Therefore we have not only an argument for the possibility of resurrection, we have a strong hope based on an event which we recall in our creed – 'On the third day he rose again'. So now we know; God has not only the will, but also the power to allow nothing, not even the death and decay of these mortal bodies of ours, to block us off from his eternal life. His love will never let us go. That is why we Christians believe in a life to come.

Conclusion

Let me end with a story. It is told by Felice Holman in a book published in 1983 called *The Wild Children*. It is about a twelve-year old Russian boy called Alex in Moscow. His parents had been snatched away from home by the secret police never to be seen again. It happened to tens, if not hundreds of thousands. This was in 1923. As a result hordes of destitute children lived together in gangs keeping alive by the only way possible to them – stealing. They were called the *Bezprizorni*, or Wild Children. Alex, however, finding himself destitute, fled instead to his school-teacher, Ekaterina, and she, brave woman, housed him as long as she dared. But finally he too was forced to join the great army of 'Wild Children'. But she never forgot him. She did not forget him when she escaped to Finland herself, and against terrible odds she arranged his escape with some other Wild Boys across the sea to safety. And when he, Alex, scrambled out of the boat on the other side, he could scarcely believe his eyes. There stood Ekaterina, his old school-teacher, waiting with open arms. So life began again.

Is this a little how it will be when we make our final journey from this life across to the other side? 'Thou shalt guide me with thy counsel and after that receive me with glory.' ' " 'I am the God of Abraham, the God of Isaac, and the God of

106

Jacob.' God is not God of the dead but of the living." The people heard what he said, and were astounded at his teaching.'

21. Not Even a Resurrection

Luke 16.31 (JB)   *If they will not listen either to Moses or to the prophets, they will not be convinced even if someone should rise from the dead.*

Every good story ends with a punch line. Today we have a good story. It was read for the gospel and it, too, ends with a punch line. If, however, we fail to recognize that the punch line comes at the end we shall start running round with the misconception that the story aims to give us a preview of hell; or even worse, what is to be the fate of all rich men; and this would be a travesty of the truth.

1. Who is the rich man?

Let me retell the story. Here is a rich man. *Immediately* you cease to pay attention on the grounds that you are not rich, and so the story has no message for you. Maybe you are not rich in financial terms, but nor am I. Are you nevertheless sure that you are not rich in other ways? Have we not received a good education? so good that we do not mooch along in the seamy grooves of sexy magazines and strip cartoons, unable to appreciate anything higher? – literature, painting, sculpture, music, even opera? Of course the rich man in the story ought never to have pulled down the blinds of his carriage so as to avoid seeing the wretch at his gate covered with sores, but do we not look down *our* noses at the vast ill-educated masses wallowing in their pornography and glue-sniffing, ignorant even of the names of such giants as Mozart, Michelangelo, Murillo and Milton?

Some of us are rich in married happiness, healthy families, children doing well. It is so easy to shrug our shoulders over the poverty of those deprived of genuine love. O, the unkindness for instance of some of the remarks made about middle-aged spinsters! And do the rich in affection never give a

107

thought to those whose lives are eked out in loneliness, anxious over what their declining years hold? And the unwanted children, the weekend children; this weekend with this set of parents, next weekend with that? All right, the average child aged fourteen and fifteen (we are told) spends each week £5.13 pocket money. I had one penny (old coinage) at that age, but I had love, security and significance. I was rich.

Yes we look out on these love-starved people, shrug our shoulders and wonder what we can do anyway for this sorry crowd in modern Britain. Do not I catch myself saying time and time again as I read in the newspapers of yet another case of drug abuse, sexual assault, marriage break-up and child abuse – what can you expect? But what can *I* do? What indeed? I can at least refrain from asserting that I am in no sense a rich man and therefore this story which Jesus told of the rich man and Lazarus has nothing to say to me.

2. *The limits of miracle*

The story then changes gear and before you know where you are death has intervened, and both the rich man and Lazarus are there on the other side of the curtain of our mortality; only this time their fortunes are reversed. The rich man is in misery and the poor man is in bliss. And up go the cheers of the bitter with society who hear this story. This is how it should be! All the rich, who of course are wicked, thrust down to hell, and all the poor who of course are good, raised up to heaven! What is more, the fact that Jesus told this story puts him into the category of the real revolutionary, even a Marxist foreshadowed.

All this is to stand the story on its head. The rich are not all bad, and the poor are not all good. The trouble with this rich man in this story was that he never thought about anything else except his riches. That is to say, he cared for nothing and no one except his life-style. But then suprisingly he remembered something! He remembered some*one*. But it was too late. He was 'on the other side' by then. He remembered his five brothers, a spark of concern for their welfare was even kindled in him: 'Bid Lazarus' he cried to Abraham, 'Bid Lazarus go and tell them not to live as I have lived, cosseted and comfortable in my own cushioned life-style with never a care for others; tell them lest they also make a hell of their own existence. Hell is emptiness; no love, no joy, no heartwarming hope, nothing but disillusionment and undying distaste. Tell my brothers, Abraham; warn them Abraham; though I confess it will take some doing, they are so sunk in their secularism, materialism and politicizing of almost everything they touch. A mighty manifestation of miraculous proportion will be necessary to make them listen, so I suggest that Lazarus be resurrected from the dead and go and tell them the truth about life. They will pay heed to a resurrection.'

And then I suppose there was a long pause. Abraham stood there looking at the rich man and finally said, 'No, they have Moses and the prophets, let them listen to them'. And then the rich man thought of the ordinariness of his sabbath worship, how dull much of it was, how pedestrian. Dragged hymns, dull sermon! So he protested, 'Ah, no Abraham, if someone comes to them from the dead, they will repent, they will change their minds.' And again Abraham shook his head. 'No' he replied, 'if they will not listen to Moses or the prophets, they will not be convinced even if someone should rise from the dead.'

And that, of course, is the punch-line of this story which comes right at the end. And it is the text of this sermon because these are the words that carry the message of the gospel reading for today. The stupendous, even the miraculous, is ineffective for evoking faith and changing people radically.

3. The resurrection of Jesus

But are we not often in the same mind as the rich man? We look out on our unhappy world today. Disillusionment abounds; for many, misery and torment. If only God would do

something, something really big to make people see for
themselves that peace not war, love not hate, giving not
getting, is the way to contentment. If only God would do
something then we should see a mighty repentance in the land,
law and order would ensue and this creeping cruelty and
callowness would wither away. O God, we need a miracle, a
mighty big miracle.

But God, as it were, shakes his head and says 'No! If people
do not believe because of what I have already given, this lovely
world, the incarnation of Jesus of Nazareth, and the witness of
saints and martyrs down the ages, they will not be convinced
by a miracle now. I'll tell you what would happen. Before the
day was out they would have found a rational explanation
(so-called) of the miracle; or they would be so knocked out
mentally by the marvel that nothing like reasonable faith
would ever be possible.'

And before we close the book and shut down the story with
the punch line, let us recall that God did accomplish one
utterly unique miracle – he brought back Jesus of Nazareth
from the dead. Therein lies the gospel. Therein lies the good
news for our temporal and eternal welfare. But the risen Christ
did not go and stand on the pinnacle of the temple for all to see.
He did not go striding into Pilate who had ordered his
crucifixion and cry 'There now, who was right, you or I?' He
was seen only by those who believed in him.

No! startling action does not evoke faith. It is only in
quietness and complete freedom from compulsion, be it
physical or psychological, that faith arises, and usually through
love of a person. So Abraham says to us in effect, and God
says, 'Look, you have your parish church, you have your
eucharist, you have your Bible, you have the lives of good men
and women around you, some rich, some poor, some not so
rich, some not so poor, who do not pull down the blinds lest
they be disturbed by those less fortunate than themselves. If
you do not believe because of them, you wouldn't be convinced
if one came back from the dead. So make sure you build on
what you have, and keep it safe for the generations that come

after. It makes for life eternal.' It is all here in Godstone.* All the good news of Jesus Christ is here in Godstone Sunday by Sunday.

* In Surrey where this sermon was preached.

22. The Defeat of Pessimism

1 Corinthians 15.54   *Death is swallowed up in victory.*

On 3 April 1987 I listened to an anthem broadcast from
Worcester Cathedral entitled *Exile* by Sumsion. I had never
heard it before but for days on end bits of the music stuck in
my mind and I caught myself singing it, or more accurately,
trying to sing it. It was a musical arrangement of that plaintive
and haunting psalm which reads,

> By the waters of Babylon we sat down and wept:
> when we remembered thee, O Sion.
> As for our harps, we hanged them up:
> upon the trees that are therein.

When the anthem opened you could hear the water lapping
softly and endlessly as the river flowed timelessly by. Its
undulations were always there. Day and night they were there.
There was nothing else. Always the water. Always the lapping.
You can't sing in a situation like that, it gets you down. There
is no point in doing anything; life loses its meaning when there
seems no end to this remorseless captivity.

> By the waters of Babylon we sat down and wept:
> when we remembered thee, O Sion.
> As for our harps, we hanged them up:
> upon the trees that are therein.
> For they that led us away captive required of us
> then a song, and melody in our heaviness:
> Sing us one of the songs of Sion.
> How shall we sing the Lord's song:
> in a strange land?

1. Prevailing pessimism

I don't know why this doleful music should have made such an
impression on me. I expect it was because I had been listening

112

to the daily news bulletins – more killings in Northern Ireland, more devastation in Lebanon, no respite in the seven years Iran–Iraq war. The terror goes on and on, and we lose heart. What is worse we don't really listen any more to those who offer solutions to our human predicament. That is the trouble; there aren't any solutions. This is how life is, was, and always will be; a sorry business. Ideals are dead. No happy endings are in sight, and worse still, never will be.

By the waters of Babylon we sat down and wept: when we remembered thee, O Sion.

Was it I that was at fault? Was I having a temporary 'fit of the blues' that Friday on 3 April 1987? Or had I slipped back, only temporarily I trust, from my Christian faith into the prevailing mood of the twentieth century? It is a mood contaminated by World War II – Belsen, Dachau, Maidanek where one-and-a-half million people were exterminated, cremated and their ashes used as fertilizers – and when that was all over, the Gulag Archipelago and the threat of nuclear war. Is it any wonder we can't take Victorian novels any more with their happy endings. Life as we know it has very few happy endings. Marriages today scarcely even have happing *beginnings*, for the escape-hatch of divorce after once year is ready and waiting, and thousands sooner or later take advantage of it. So where is the fun now? Life is a sorry affair and the best we can hope for is to catch what glimpses of sunshine there are on the way; or 'go the pace' and damn the consequences. Nothing matters except to get what you can. Thus violence, thus vandalism, thus terrorism. Thus the last quarter of the twentieth century.

And here in the midst of this bizarre futility stands the Church preaching a gospel of resurrection which appears no less bizarre because it is not pessimistic but the reverse. So Easter is laughed at as they laughed at it in Athens nineteen centuries ago when Paul preached the risen Christ. More likely the gospels, which tell of his resurrection, are rejected out of hand for no other reason than that they seem to savour of a happy ending. Or, as a kind of halfway stage, the crucifixion of

Jesus is accepted, even revered, because it shows what life is like – not even the best of men escape suffering because that is how life is. All right then, we will have Good Friday, but please, not Easter; it does not square with our experience.

And as I recite this sorry, pessimistic story I sense a rising protest among my hearers. But life isn't all miserable! There are flowers around, and glorious spring days, and lambs gambolling in the fields. There is music and dancing. There are thousands upon thousands deriving satisfaction from DIY (including your preacher!). And for some, scoring goals at football and millions more watching them being scored. And the joy of bringing off an ace service at tennis. Can it really be that all this beauty, all this pleasure is in the world simply to mock us? We feel in our bones this pessimistic view must be wrong. Granted there is suffering in life, but there is also joy; there is pain, but there is also pleasure; evil but there is also good. Is it not as reasonable, therefore, to take an optimistic view as a pessimistic view? Of course you cannot prove the one or the other, but surely this much is clear, pessimism is not the only philosophy which thinking men and women must assume.

2. A breakthrough

And so we pick up the gospel narrative again and do not stop short at the resurrection of Jesus as if it were some kind of happy ending. Curiously enough, or perhaps not curiously at all, the background of the resurrection events is a pessimism as all-pervading as that which is in vogue today. Jesus was dead. The man who had it in him to lead the nation out of the social and political morass in which it was trapped had been executed, revealing an apparent powerlessness when the crunch came no different at worst from a slave, nor different at best from any other idealist. Seeing that happen to *this* man, his followers had no hope left. The world must be as rotten as in their worst moments they had thought it must be. Pessimism ruled their day. Yes, I will admit that, if not then, at some time the more thoughtful would have read glory into the tragedy. Here was a good man dying for ideals, so ideals had witness borne to their nobility, permanent witness. Tragedy can convey this consolation. Were it bereft of any message, the world's great tragedians would never have commanded a theatre. Such a subtle insight was not, however, evident on Good Friday. The shallow sightseers returning from Golgotha beating their breasts illustrated their pessimism. If the world can wish to be rid of such a man as Jesus, it must be the rotten old world we often half thought it was. There was no optimism in the air when Easter dawned.

And then the unexpected happened: Christ rose from the dead. I know some people, some Christians even, reckon this resurrection took place only in the minds of his followers, that is to say there grew up a new way of thinking about him and henceforth his would be a spiritual presence. I concede that this interpretation, though unorthodox, does still carry a gospel of resurrection. What I find difficult is to see how it could have been generated given the climate of pessimism that prevailed.

I am also ready to agree that in the midst of the pessimism the hope of happiness was not completely dead. It lay dormant in the hearts of men and women everywhere, sustained even by prophets and thinkers; but the smoky flame would never have flared up so quickly into a shining light had not something startling happened. That something was, I believe, the resurrection of Christ from the grave.

And what does it say? It says death is not the end. Indeed Easter proclaims the death of death, a phrase I culled recently from the title of a book by one called Otto Riethmüller, *Das Todes Tod*. Death is our last enemy. It is our direst enemy. We cannot beat it. Sooner or later it will 'get us all'. Oh yes, strong men will laugh it off, but only because they are afraid of it too, and have no wish to admit it.

> The old grey hearse goes rumbling by
> And we don't know whether to laugh or cry.

But death was defeated on Easter Day. Easter Day is Victory Day. Easter Day is optimistic day. *It signals the death of pessimism*; pessimism about what is going to happen to this old world of ours; pessimism about the survival of ideals; pessimism about the sanctity of human life; pessimism about standards; pessimism about morality; pessimism about tomorrow. The sun will shine again and the trees will blossom! 'Death is swallowed up in victory'. This is what Easter says. Pessimism is doomed.

3. Easter Christians

Perhaps this theme is nowhere more strikingly illustrated than in the forty miles or so of catacombs or underground passages that remain to the north east and south of Rome's city walls. It was there that the Roman Christians of the fourth century buried their dead confident that the authorities, even in their persecution phase, would not molest them. What is remarkable is the strong contrast between the inscriptions on those tombs and those in a typical pagan cemetery called a Necropolis; that is, city of the dead. A Necropolis is a place of unrelieved gloom. The words *Vale*, 'Farewell' dominate the scene, telling, maybe, of stoical courage in the face of death but certainly not of hope. But in the catacombs there is no gloom. The departed are named with a delicacy of affection and confidence in the future because of the risen Christ who is their Good Shepherd. It is not too much to say that everything in the catacombs is stamped with victory.

In the light of this I think sometimes I would like to coin a new phrase. Perhaps someone has coined it already, I don't know. It would be 'Easter Christians'. These would be the buoyant ones, the cheerful ones, the optimistic ones, the Christians who never dwell on the black side and never load their own troubles on to other people uninvited. Such Christians exist. And do not imagine they are the ones always brimful of abundant health or whose lives are cushioned with wealth. Indeed it is not rare to find the most fortunate the most miserable. No, Easter Christians are those who triumph over adversity and are a benediction to meet. They have died to self with Christ and they have risen with him. If only the whole Church shone with that life and liveliness. What an acted sermon it would be in a pessimistic age. Easter Christians! 'Death is swallowed up in victory' (1 Corinthians 15.54).

23.   The Risen Christ's Commission

Matthew 28.18–20 (NEB)   *Jesus then came up and spoke to them. He said: 'Full authority in heaven and on earth has been committed to me. Go forth therefore and make all nations my disciples; baptize men everywhere in the name of the Father and the Son and the Holy Spirit, and teach them to observe all that I have commanded you. And be assured I am with you always, to the end of time.'*

This doesn't sound a bit like Jesus. Judging from his speech in the gospels this formal style is not how he ever spoke to his disciples. It is more like an address at a public meeting. And what about this phrase, 'in the name of the Father and the Son and the Holy Spirit'? Has it not an ecclesiastical ring about it? And did not the early Church for decades, if not a century or two, baptize converts in the simple name of 'Jesus Christ our Lord'? It was a long time before this Trinitarian formula was devised.

So what shall we do? Reject these verses altogether? But have they not been called 'The Great Commission', and acted as the scriptural charter for hundreds and hundreds of Christian missionaries who have gone abroad making disciples of Christ and founding churches? What is more, have not a goodly company of both men and women given their lives in response to what has been accepted as a royal command, more particularly as it occurs in the verses that were added to St Mark's Gospel, 'Go ye into all the world and preach the gospel to every creature'?

No, on no account must these verses be rejected. For all their formal un-Christlike *style* of utterance they are thoroughly Christlike in content. Indeed, they epitomize what must be the consequence of all who accept that Christ is risen. We must go forth and tell the good news to all who will hear it. We must make disciples near and far. We must impart Christ's teaching, and we must live in the light of his continual presence with us till the end of time as we engage in this mission.

But what about this style of utterance? Look at it this way. Here is St Matthew writing towards the end of the first century. His gospel, unlike St Mark's, is not an interpreted eyewitness account of the swift-moving life of Jesus, but rather a structured presentation of his teaching ministry employing such literary sources and traditions as were available to him (including St Mark's gospel), all edited and designed for the use of the early Church. And in the last verses of his book he set out in dramatic form whence the impetus came for all that the Church was doing in its missionary enterprise. It stemmed from the risen Christ and the authorization and instructions he left with his apostles. St Matthew summarized this *in his own words and style* as we have it in Matthew 28.18-20. We can confidently read here what the risen Lord would have us do.

1. The call to evangelize

First we are to make disciples. Some churches, alas, seem to have lost all missionary thrust. Instead they give the appearance of being content merely to maintain their own tradition. It is as if they are saying 'Well, the church is here, people can come to it if they wish to, and they will be expected to fit in with the way we do things.' But this complacency is leagues away from the risen Christ's commission to the apostles – 'Go forth therefore.' We are expected to be outreaching, outgoing and enterprising. It is easy for our contemporary Church in Britain, absorbed in structural revision and acutely sensitive about social welfare, to write off the great missionary movement of the Victorian Church as covert colonialism. Of course its paternalistic style was unfortunate, to say the least, but it did act upon the command of the risen Christ 'Go forth therefore and make all nations my disciples'. Has there ever been an outreach of the Christian Church like that of the nineteenth century? And it is easy to reckon that because we now recognize true insights into the nature of reality on the part of religions other than Christianity that Christ has no uniqueness and therefore ought not to be preached. When the Church loses its obligations to evangelize however it dies on its feet.

Britain needs evangelism today. Morally and spiritually it has drifted further and further into a grey area of uncertainty over the meaning of life altogether. The nation is appalled at the breakdown of law and order but knows no way of arresting the decline. Increased social benefits, however right and proper, are not the answer. It is the soul of the community that needs healing and that is precisely where the ministry of the Church is called to operate – 'Go forth therefore and make disciples . . .' This is the command of the risen Christ.

We do well to observe that there is nothing vague about this evangelism. Disciples are to be gathered *into the Church*. Exhortation to good behaviour is not evangelism. There needs to be commitment to the risen Christ, which means as much of him as we are able to grasp; we are not all called to be theologians. And the commitment needs to be sealed in baptism, baptism into (St Matthew's word) the name of the Father, the Son and the Holy Spirit, and this gives entry into Christ's family, the Church, and membership of it. This is elementary: it is basic. When the apostles went forth, notably St Peter and St Paul, they did not only proclaim Christ risen, they gathered into churches those who committed themselves to this faith, providing for them a ministry at the same time. Evangelism without church, that is congregation building, leaves little if any permanent mark.

2. *The call to teach*

Secondly the churches are to be taught. They are to have imparted to them the teaching of Jesus. If there is to be an evangelistic ministry there must also be a teaching ministry. After the great evangelical revivals of the late nineteenth century, led chiefly by those two most unlikely evangelists for England, the Americans Moody and Sankey, responsible for the conversion of thousands to the Christian faith, it is no accident that able Christian teachers arose. Dr Campbell Morgan, minister of Buckingham Gate Congregational Church in London, was an outstanding example. It was during this period too that church building went on apace. Moody and Sankey will not, in all probability, be our style, indeed they would fit ill in the modern world; and the kind of teaching which nurtured their converts would be questioned today; the clock cannot be put back. Nevertheless, the Church needs teaching. Unfortunately it cannot be said that the Church of our day is strong in this area of its life. Even preaching, which is not exactly teaching, has been under a cloud for decades. We have congregations today far smaller than they used to be, and far from being moderately informed about what the Christian faith actually teaches.

Part of our trouble is that we are desperately afraid of authority. We have become so bewitched with the democratic idea and with the concept of universal participation that we would almost like an election among church people as to what is to be believed and what rejected. St Matthew in our text for today will have none of this. On the contrary he is quite categorical. The risen Christ instructed his apostles to teach the church believers 'to observe all that I have commanded you'. No, we do not believe in an infallible Church and we do not believe in an infallible Bible but we do, or we should, look to the mind of Christ as authoritative for what we are to believe and do.

Is this easy? Who said this was easy? The Old Testament standard of behaviour is much more acceptable to most people. I was waiting my turn at a delicatessen counter the other day when two women began discussing the two cases of men who had falsely reported that they had lost relatives in the ferry disaster at Zeebrugge, in order to obtain the compensation available to victims. They thought the men ought to be rowed out in a boat and sunk beside the stricken vessel! There it is, 'an eye for an eye and a tooth for a tooth'. Christ said however, when someone strikes you on the one cheek offer him the other also. And not only did he endorse the ten commandments, he stiffened their application. Hate is equivalent to murder, the adulterous look to the immoral act. And who is willing to hear his strictures on divorce? That the sincere Christian minister should shrink from proclaiming Christ's teaching is understandable; after all, can he wholly escape being guilty himself? What he must remember, however, is that what he has to impart is not his own teaching but Christ's, and he himself stands under its judgement even while he imparts it.

Yet there is a strange authority when Christ's teaching is conveyed which does not appear to belong to any other form of Christian instruction. What is more, people respond to authority, they look for it, they feel safer with it. It is doubtful whether any saving activity of any kind is possible in the absence of authority. So the Church needs the authority of Christ. Its teaching activity needs to be based there. Could it be that the Church is failing because it has become uncertain of its teaching role?

3.   The assurance of the divine presence

Making disciples and teaching disciples did not constitute the sole content of the risen Christ's commission to his apostles, there was also the assurance of his divine presence. 'And be assured', he said, 'I am with you always to the end of time.' What a relief this is! What a heartening promise! The Christian way is at times very rough, the opposition formidable; but we need not be afraid, we need not give up hope. Christ is with us always, the risen Christ. He is the Lord and he cares for us.

One of the most attractive stories I heard many years ago concerned one of our most famous wartime BBC news readers; his name was on everyone's lips; we hung on his words. It was at the time of the evacuation of East London because of the heavy German bombing raids. This distinguished man somehow heard how one woman was embarrassed to join with the other women from her street because she had no one to see her off at the station. So he volunteered, and as she passed through the barrier (it could have been Paddington), he was there and called out in a loud voice for everyone to hear, 'Goodbye, darling, goodbye. I'll be thinking of you'. And the woman went on her way with a courage that would otherwise have been non-existent.

The consciousness of someone's thought of us at the difficult moments of life is reassuring. Loneliness, with no one who cares, is one of the hardest burdens to carry. What strength then is there that the risen Christ assured his Church of his presence till the end of time. We are not deserted. We are not forgotten. We are not struggling alone. Granted, it is an unseen presence, but taken even at its lowest level, who is there seriously ill that has not been sustained by the knowledge that friends are thinking of them, and perhaps praying for them; and the spiritual presence of the risen Christ is dynamic on a higher level altogether! At the end of the day it is not explanations of life that we need but the consciousness of God's presence with us. 'Yea, though I walk through the valley of the shadow of death, I will fear no evil: for thou art with me.' This was the promise the risen Christ gave with his great commission. We go out into the world in his name, but we do not go alone.

24. A New Song

Revelation 5.9, 12   *And they sing a new song . . . Worthy
is the Lamb that hath been slain to receive the power, and
riches, and wisdom, and might, and honour, and glory, and
blessing.*

If you have ever sung in a choral society – and I have, and I
guess some of you have too – you will know how difficult it is
merely to *say* the words of this text, because the music to
which Handel set them in his *Messiah* will keep ringing in our
ears. But how remarkable that the author of the book called
Revelation should have had a song ringing in his ears at all! He
was a prisoner in a slave camp on the rocky island of Patmos, a
bare thirteen miles square in the Aegean sea a few miles from
the mainland of Asia Minor. According to the Roman historian
Pliny it was used by the Romans as a penal settlement. Life
was harsh there, even brutal. Labour camps are notoriously so.
Don't we know in our modern world?

1. A song in prison

It was Sunday when this author, John, heard this song in his
heart and wrote down the words. It was the weekly commemo-
ration of Easter when, over on the mainland, the seven
churches he knew so well would be assembling to sing the
praise of the risen Christ, and he could not be there. He was a
prisoner. His crime was that he confessed Jesus as Lord, the
only One to be worshipped, and not Domitian the Emperor.
Nor all the Roman emperors took their divinity seriously but
this one did. He reigned from AD 81–AD 96. He insisted that
he be called 'Our Lord and God', and executed or banished
those who would not conform; even members of his own
family. Perhaps Emperor worship strikes us as odd but not so
long ago it was enforced in Japan as a means of binding the
nation together in the absence of one common religion. This

124

was the aim of Emperor worship in Rome's far-flung empire, embracing a bewildering variety of races, religions and cultures. A political device it no doubt was, but the Christians felt they could not compromise their faith. They recognized as Lord and God the risen Christ, not the Emperor Domitian. So they were persecuted; and John, the author of Revelation, found himself, as he writes in his book (1.9), 'on the isle of Patmos for the word of God and the testimony of Jesus'. It was only fifty years ago that Christian pastors in Germany also found themselves in a no-compromise situation when they were ordered by the state to exclude from their fellowship any believers of Jewish origin.

Would you have a song in your heart in a situation like that? Would the words of a new song spring up in your mind when every bone in your body seemed broken by the grinding brutality of the taskmaster's whip? But they did in John's mind, the author of the Revelation. That is the first marvel of what he has to tell in his book; 'And they sung a new song', the saints of God in heaven round about the throne – 'Worthy is the Lamb that hath been slain to receive the power, and riches, and wisdom, and might and honour and glory and blessing.' Look at these saints on earth and you will see the marks of the lash across their backs, the terrible blisters on their hands, men who were once upright but are now hobbling and broken; and all because, like John, they would go on preaching the Lordship of the risen Christ whatever edicts Domitian, the emperor, might promulgate.

There can't be much of an Easter faith in yours and my heart unless a song of some kind is not far away from our lips. There can't be a Christian congregation, there can't be Christian worship, without singing, however cracked the voices may be. The fact that Christ is risen necessitates singing. Songs of praise there have to be. And how uplifting they are! Think of the enormous popularity of the BBC programme that goes by this name on Sundays! It tells its own story. The Christian faith is a buoyant faith because at its heart is resurrection; in the future, yes, but in the little deaths of our life experience now, on the way. It shines even in the dark, indeed the dark never blots it out. That is why there is always a song in the Church, it is because Christ is risen.

2. God's world

But as John looked around him did it appear as if Christ were Lord whether risen or not? Everything about his surroundings cried aloud that Domitian was Lord, the State was supreme. And has it not always appeared so? Egypt, Babylon, Greece, Rome, Nazi Germany, Marxist Russia; these are the powers that rule the world. But will it always be so? Have not all these giants feet of clay? Have we not read of how they eventually crumbled, even when in some cases they had lasted so long it is not surprising that generation after generation of people suffering them looked on them as permanent? But not the prophets in the Old Testament, and not John on the isle of Patmos in the New Testament. They saw a time when the kingdoms of the world shall become the Kingdom of the Lord Christ who shall reign for ever and ever. The rise of all earthly powers is not a cyclical pattern that goes on perpetually, there will come an end; history is working towards an end, when we do not know, but the message of the risen Christ is that he will in the end be seen to be what he in fact is; Lord of eternity and of this world.

There is a kind of earthiness about this part of the Easter preaching, but we need to grasp it. This is God's world. He is the Creator of it and the sustainer of it. Without God it would not be. Not surprisingly, therefore, the beauty of the earth, its order and its harmony, perhaps in some strange way even its disharmony, may become for us mediators of the nature of God; some would use the word 'sacramental'. All of which being so, can we imagine that God has no *ultimate* use for it? Can we think that God would allow man wholly to destroy it by whatever sophisticated tools he may have invented? But wouldn't this make man king of the world and not God? The

God of the resurrection is the God of creation. He will resurrect what he has made. This is why some of us do not doubt that Jesus' tomb really was found to be empty on Easter morning as the scriptures aver. The resurrection of Jesus was not simply a spiritual affair, the body being left to decompose with the passage of time. No, *his body* was transmuted, showing that matter is not waste material but is to be taken up in God's ultimate purpose for this world. As the womb of Mary was not *abhorred* (to use the word which the Te Deum uses) but was used in the Incarnation, a material body, to achieve God's purpose: so the body of Jesus was not abandoned in the resurrection and only his spirit raised: this shows what is God's final purpose for the world.

Is this hard to believe? Of course it is hard to believe. It is also hard to express in imaginable terms, and even more difficult to avoid theological phraseology. The preacher is in a real dilemma here. But he must have a message with a future in it or it will fall very far short of what the New Testament promises.

> Christ has died
> Christ is risen
> Christ will come again.

3. *Concern for eternity and time*

What then are we to do about it? How are we to live in the light of this future when the kingdoms of the world shall become the Kingdom of the Lord Christ? Sit down and do nothing? Make no effort at all to right the glaring wrongs of this world? Stand back from attempting to make this world a better place? Refuse to engage in politics which are the instruments for social action? Adopt a policy of non-cooperation with any government?

There are two main reactions, both extreme. One is to throw our total effort into building the Kingdom of God here on earth, just as if we can. The Kingdom of the Lord Christ is the

128

pattern with which *we* are to work. In the high mediaeval period of European history there was a belief that the religious and the political could be completely harmonized in a kind of theocracy. Today there is a belief that the achievement of total justice by political action is the first work of the Church. Over against this view and completely opposed to it is the conviction that the Church must be free of every kind of involvement, or even concern, for things political. Both these views are extreme and unrealistic. Christian wisdom advises that we follow the underlying thought of the great Church Father, Augustine, Bishop of Hippo. The Church is to have its eye first on the Kingdom of God, the perfect Kingdom of the Lord Christ which he alone can make in the future but it must also encourage as much of that Kingdom's compassion and justice as may be possible in the here and now. We cannot, being sinful men and women, caught in a sinful network, ever fashion Utopia; but we must not be pessimistic and do nothing. We must do what we can, using such means as may be available and workable at the time; and what we do will not be wasted. It will be gathered up in God's eternal Kingdom of his future which is to come.

Does this put a song in our hearts? Let us be honest. Not at once. Too often the skies are too grey for any but the most superficial to be immediately, if ever, bubbling over with excitement. I doubt if John on the island of Patmos, his chain clanking with the clanking of his fellow prisoners in the labour camp, shouted for joy very often. But he knew the future was safe in the hands of the risen Christ who one day would reign. Then perhaps he whistled occasionally as he quarried those awful slates, if that is what he was forced to do. 'Worthy is the Lamb that hath been slain, to receive the power, and riches, and wisdom, and might, and honour and glory and blessing.' Even so come Lord Jesus. Amen.